HIDDEN METRICS

THE COACH'S SECRET to SUCCESS that REALLY MATTERS

M. NORA BOUCHARD

Bouchard Executive Coaching Ltd.
www.mnorabouchard.com
admin@mnorabouchard.com

ORDERING INFORMATION
Quantity Sales: Special discounts are available on quantity purchase by corporations, associations, and others. For details, contact admin@mnorabouchard.com. Individual Sales: This book is available through most bookstores or can be ordered directly from BEC Ltd. Contact www.hidden-metrics.com.

Distributed in the United States by IngramSpark.

Library of Congress Cataloging in Publication Control Room:
9798993123707

Cover design and text design by Elsa Safir
Interior illustrations by Sunshine BenBelkacem
Content and Line Level Editing by Erin McClary
Proofreading by thinkStory.biz

ISBN: 979-8-9931237-0-7

Also by Nora
Mayday! Asking for Help in Times of Need
By M. Nora Klaver
BERRETT-KOEHLER PUBLISHERS

This book is dedicated to Pierre, the LOML.

CONTENTS

INTRODUCTION: THE COACH'S SECRET

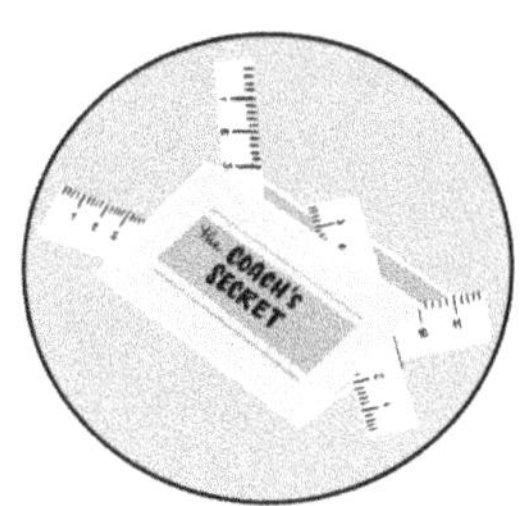

> A FOCUS ON MEASURABLE PERFORMANCE INDICATORS CAN LEAD MANAGERS TO NEGLECT TASKS FOR WHICH NO CLEAR MEASURES OF PERFORMANCE ARE AVAILABLE... UNABLE TO COUNT INTANGIBLE ASSETS SUCH AS REPUTATION, EMPLOYEE SATISFACTION, MOTIVATION, LOYALTY, TRUST, AND COOPERATION, THOSE ENAMORED OF PERFORMANCE METRICS SQUEEZE ASSETS IN THE SHORT TERM AT THE EXPENSE OF LONG-TERM CONSEQUENCES.
> — JERRY Z. MULLER, *The Tyranny of Metrics*

There's a secret I'm going to share with you. It's something that most corporate coaches do but rarely tell anyone about. We keep it quiet, hidden, for reasons that will soon become clear.

This secret is part of the magic that is coaching. Though, to be honest, coaching isn't magical. It is a set of specific, rigorous skills designed to reveal the wisdom that is already inside you. It may feel like magic to our clients, but it's not.

What is this coaching secret? Let me tell you. When you and I sit down together to refine your goals, we often overlook the goals set by your supervisors or bosses and secretly craft new ones.

Shocking, I know!

Why? Because together, we often discover something is missing from the prescribed goals and metrics that are handed down to us by your leaders. These assigned goals can be superficial and outward-facing. What is missing are the special, deep, vital targets that lead to personal and professional fulfillment. Because they are so individual, we keep them on the QT, private, undisclosed, and secret from your manager.

Organizations hire coaches for a myriad of reasons. Initially, when I first began coaching thirty years ago, it was to help build skills. Back then, the decision-makers or sponsors of coaching had a limited understanding of how coaching works and its potential effectiveness. Most assumed it was to improve presentation skills only. Later, sponsors brought in coaches to "fix" leaders who got results but were toxic for the organization. I coached many "alpha" leaders who, by nature, were demanding and intimidating, and I helped them modify their approach to be more collaborative and supportive. Every professional coach I know has resisted this kind of work, however. We don't appreciate using our hard-earned skills to "fix" people. And it certainly doesn't invite others to want to work with a professional coach if the client thinks I'm there to repair something that is broken.

Thankfully, after three decades, I see organizations using coaches the way they should be used: to build and deepen leadership through a positive focus on meaning and strengths. Nowadays, companies bring us in to improve awareness of self and others, achieve personal and professional goals, make better decisions, improve performance, harness influence, establish solid reputations, build better work/life balance, create stronger relationships, enhance team dynamics, set and implement visions, apply strengths, communicate more effectively, and stay accountable.

Over time, professional corporate coaches have become true and valued learning partners in developing leaders, teams, and individual contributors.

Throughout this book, you will read stories of how I've coached my clients on a variety of topics. You'll see how each coachee made personal discoveries and turned them into tangible outcomes that accelerated their leadership and careers.

If you have missed out on working with a professional coach, what you may not know is that the coaching process operates at a deeper level than most realize. Our work is driven by what matters to the client, not just what the organization needs. The company benefits, to be sure, but it's the individual who walks away transformed.

Allow me a moment to tell you how executive or leadership coaches typically begin our engagements. First, we meet with the individual's supervisor and the human resource business partner (HRBP). This meeting is sometimes referred to as a "situational analysis." In these conversations, we learn about the intended goals of the coaching engagement, as well as the changes or growth management wants the individual to achieve. We discuss possible action steps, timelines, and measurements of success (i.e., metrics). Pretty straightforward.

These initial goals are typically set based on the requirements of the role and function. They may be adjusted somewhat to also address some of the individual's specific challenges. However, these "assigned goals" are simply starting points—the minimum management wants to achieve with you and your coach.

I'm not a big fan of these goals. I find assigned goals to be dry, basic, vague, or just too obvious. It's the easy-to-track stuff: delivering work product, making sure the team hits its deadlines, rolling out a new initiative, getting along with colleagues better, etc. My opinion notwithstanding, I wholeheartedly agree that these are all legitimate goals and worth achieving. As a professional and ethical coach, I will ensure we reach them, if not exceed them. But all coaches feel, in our bones, that something more is possible.

Me, Myself, and I

I began my career developing training programs for a global consulting firm. That job introduced me to those who are inclined to be left-brained, logical, and methodical. As someone who tends to lean more right-brained—creative and intuitive—I found that even though I wasn't at all like my colleagues, I was able to help them see beyond their usual paradigms.

I enjoyed serving leaders around the world in Australia, Europe, Asia, Canada, and the United States. Together, we created live in-person training that addressed corporate turnaround methodologies and litigation services. Yet, developing and delivering these programs wasn't enough to satisfy me fully. I knew, deep down, I wanted to have a more significant impact on these folks and their lives.

Later, I discovered the field of coaching, which at the time was still being dismissed as something touchy-feely and unproven. Little did the nay-sayers know at the time how life-altering a coaching relationship can be.

No doubt each coach out there has a similar "aha" moment—when they observed the power of coaching and subsequently knew they wanted to be a part of it. Mine was during a presentation by two experienced coaches who demonstrated what coaching could achieve, live and unscripted. That day, I watched as their coachees changed in front of my eyes. I witnessed powerful eureka moments that could not be ignored or dismissed. These coachees saw something new that they hadn't seen before, something that changed the trajectory of their lives. I was hooked.

Weeks later, I found myself sitting in my first coaching workshop. Before I finished the program, I had signed an agreement to coach twenty-four people on a marketing team. This was my path, I was sure of it. I've never looked back.

Since then, I've taken hundreds of hours of coaching training through various qualified organizations, like the Co-Active Training

Institute and the Newfield Network. These programs challenged me to unlearn what I had learned and to adopt new ways of seeing the world. I found that my coaching certification program through the Newfield Network was more rigorous than my master's program. When I was starting out as a coach, universities hadn't yet discovered coaching. Now you can find college-level programs to earn a coaching degree.

In addition to formal training and observation, I have over ten thousand hours and thirty years of experience sitting in the coaching chair.

Amazing coaches have also coached me. I've learned a great deal from these sessions, including how to challenge my own methodologies and be a more effective coach.

At its core, coaching is a powerful partnership that enhances, elevates, and expands on what my clients already do well. It's a life-changing process that leaves the coachee feeling amazed at what can be achieved.

How does coaching accomplish this? First, coaching is not about advice or telling someone what to do. I have yet to meet a grown adult who will take advice. (Have you? No.) Coaching is grounded in the skills of: 1) listening to more than just the surface reply and 2) asking powerful, intuitive questions. Coaches are trained to shut up and listen.

"Telling" is a hard habit to unlearn. So, we focus on being curious and asking the questions that bubble up inside us. Sometimes, the more ridiculous the question sounds in our heads, the more powerful it can be. Unlearning the habit of telling and learning the new habit of questioning is difficult, but setting aside one's ego can help tremendously. Focusing solely on what the client needs keeps me grounded.

Finally, it also helps to know that all coaching conversations are confidential. Coaches create safe spaces for their clients to be vulnerable, play, experiment, and use their imagination. Confidentiality is essential.

Who Is Who in Coaching?

Now that you know a bit about me and coaching, here's a quick primer on the different roles involved in a typical coaching engagement. I find that when coaches get together, even we have a hard time keeping track of who is who in our stories. So, here's a quick dictionary of the terms I use: 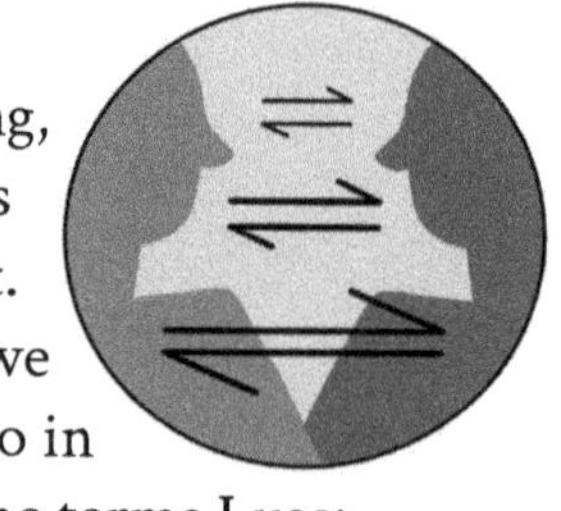

✔ **Client company:** The organization paying for coaching services.

✔ **Sponsor:** The senior-most leader who oversees the coaching engagement, contributes goal suggestions, and meets with the coach periodically to discuss progress. The sponsor also approves the coaching development plan and is present for mid-point check-ins and final meetings. Usually, the sponsor directly supervises the leader being coached.

✔ **Client:** Often referred to as the "coachee," the client is the leader participating in the coaching engagement.

✔ **Squad:** I use "squad" to differentiate those who report to you from your "team." Your squad consists of your direct reports and subsequent skip-levels. Your "squad" is not your "team."

✔ **Team:** Your team consists of your peers and your supervisor (more about this in a later chapter). Suffice it to say, your "team" is not your "squad."

✔ **Human resource business partner:** This person may participate in preliminary goal setting for the coaching engagement. This tends to happen only if they interact with the client and know them well. The HRBP may also participate in mid-point check-ins or final meetings.

✔ **Coach:** A fully trained and professionally certified leadership or executive coach who holds all client interactions in confidence while still satisfying the needs of the client company, sponsor, and HRBP. Yes, it can be a juggling act. Most professional coaches, however, manage to pull it off by focusing on common goals and fostering strong relationships with everyone involved in the coaching engagement.

Hidden Metrics Defined

Here's what I've learned after decades of coaching: The path to sustainable success isn't paved with profit-and-loss statements alone. There is a lot of hidden effort and personal drive that makes things happen, and most of it isn't observed, measured, or celebrated.

Hidden metrics are the invisible gauges you create, either alone or with your coach, to measure your progress toward living your best self at work. They represent the contributions you make that are grounded in your unique talents and abilities. Hidden metrics become a map that leads you to the most satisfying and fulfilling parts of how you give to the world through your work.

Think of hidden metrics as the dark matter of professional development—you can't always see them directly, but their gravitational pull shapes everything around them. They're the private victories, the internal shifts, the moments of growth that never make it into a performance review but fundamentally change how you lead.

Hidden metrics are the quiet drivers that stem from what is most meaningful to you, allowing you to create memories that will lift your spirits and bring a smile to your face for years to come. While the game-changing initiative you launched this year might be long forgotten, replaced by newer ones implemented by others, your hidden metrics will remain as a testament to the genuine impact you made.

Hidden metrics remain private—your secret scorecard—but they provide genuine markers for personal growth. Because of this, they keep you inspired.

Traditional business metrics—revenue, gross profit, customer retention rate, return in investment (ROI)—don't always inspire. And no wonder; they are intended to measure impersonal things. Instead, as a coach, I'd rather we acknowledge the profound impulses that naturally move people toward their highest goals. Coaches understand that executing a vision aligned with personal values and strengths is what keeps people pressing forward.

I certainly don't expect management to stop mandating more traditional goals and metrics—both conventional and hidden measures are needed—but up until now, deeper personal goals have been ignored and disregarded. It's my hope that business leaders will begin to talk openly with their direct reports about what truly matters, not only to the company's bottom line but also to its employees.

Throughout the rest of this book, you will learn how to build and implement your metrics so you can experience that personal satisfaction for years to come.

Who Is This Book For?

I've written this book for:

✔ **Emerging leaders:** Those who are managing their very first teams or are early in their leadership careers. If that's you, you have likely had little to no formal leadership training. Equally as likely, no one, including your boss, has described the changes in expectations everyone has for you at this next level. Hopefully, you may have been assigned a coach to help you transition into leadership. If not, hold on tightly to this book and use the Workbook in the back. You'll walk away with ideas for your hidden metrics to help you deal with the internal and external transitions headed your way.

✔ **Veteran leaders:** Those of you who, despite having been in the big chair for a while, may still be seeking new ways to polish your skills or stay engaged. If this is you, you probably aren't done with promotions yet either. There's always another level to reach. With each new title change, you will still encounter new requirements. And if you've never deliberately defined your leadership style, this book can help you with that. You may also want to create a few hidden metrics to meet your expectations.

✔ **Coaches:** Whether a new coach or a more experienced one, we love to learn from one another. It's my hope you will pick up a tip or two as you read along.

The Path Forward

Each chapter will take you through a series of essential steps that eventually lead to the creation of your hidden metrics.

✔ **Chapter 1:** Learn the reasons to keep your hidden metrics secret and how this secrecy creates safety as you develop and implement them.

✔ **Chapter 2:** Your promotion came with a new reality. There are a few things (maybe more than a few) to let go of before you even begin thinking about your hidden metrics. This chapter helps you understand what those are.

✔ **Chapter 3:** Whether you realize it or not, you are in a transition phase. This chapter introduces you to a valuable model to help you navigate it.

✔ **Chapter 4:** Now that you've laid the groundwork, this chapter introduces you to the hidden metrics equation.

✔ **Chapters 5, 6, and 7:** These delve into each element of the hidden metrics in more detail and provide a range of tools for your use.

✔ **Chapter 8:** This chapter presents three coaching case studies to demonstrate how all the pieces of your hidden metrics come together.

✔ **Chapters 9 and 10:** Both chapters explore the importance of key relationships essential for your long-term success.

✔ **Chapters 11 and 12:** Here I answer your "what if" questions and offer a few final considerations.

✔ **Your Workbook:** You have two options with the Workbook. Go ahead and read the entire book and then fill out the Workbook. Alternatively, you can complete these Workbook pages as you read.

The Coach's Secret

Coaches know that, inevitably, the goals set by upper management are important to *them*, not necessarily the client with whom I'm working. These goals are what your boss wants, not what speaks to you and your vision for yourself as a leader.

And here is a bonus: Coaches also know that by working on the hidden metrics that ensure the achievement of personally meaningful vision, the other, more mundane, business goals are achieved naturally. I'll prove it to you through real-life stories from actual clients.

Now, sit down, settle in. I invite you to take ownership of your future by exploring, understanding, and creating your own hidden metrics. As you read, take notes, underline, or highlight those ideas that excite you—or trigger you. That's where a lot of your learning will be.

1
SHH!

My first experience with hidden metrics came about early in my career. With a newly minted master of arts in instructional design and natural leadership abilities (or so I thought), I viewed myself as a hot-shot manager of a team of twelve. I sincerely loved the work and the people I worked with. Together, we produced enlightening and practical training for our internal clients.

I had a reputation as someone who understood the client, got things done, could identify additional work and lead a team, all the while rocking shoulder pads and pantyhose. (Yes, this was the late 1980s!)

I was rewarded with a quick promotion, which only added to my ego.

At one point, I found myself working late evening/early morning hours in Chicago to sync up with colleagues in our Sydney and Melbourne offices. The plan was for me to soon fly Down Under for a month to work with them on a needs assessment. I was excited and exhausted. I wanted to make sure this project went flawlessly.

That combination of odd hours, no sleep, and being laser-focused and perfectionistic was poisonous.

I don't remember the details—I probably blocked them out—but I do recall going on a rampage with a support group, people who were supposed to get me something to take on the plane for my meetings in Oz. I cussed and yelled. I had made five calls to the department to confirm that what I needed would be ready, and it wasn't. I was flying out in a couple of days and was more than disappointed; I was angry. I had been let down. How was I going to look if I didn't have that one element for my project?

Do you see a pattern? Me! Me! Me!

This wasn't my first outburst, however. With high expectations for myself and others, I had started to get a reputation for being a bully at work. If I didn't get the quality work product or service I needed to look good, there was going to be hell to pay.

I told myself an entirely different story. I was solely focused on getting the work done on time and under budget, which is what my bosses required of me.

I admit it. I am ashamed to say:

I was a toxic leader.

The next day, I was called into my supervisor's office. The shared services group had complained about me. Someone had to set me straight. And that person was my boss.

(As a side note, I adored my boss Don Grady, who passed away in 2014. I learned so many life lessons from Don, the most optimistic and wise leader I have ever worked with. I had never seen him angry. He had never corrected my behavior before, and I was feeling appropriately ashamed. I wasn't sure what to expect from my conversation with him.)

When I sat down at his desk, Don didn't make eye contact with me as he fiddled with something in a drawer. Without looking at me once, he asked me one simple question, "What are you afraid of, Nora?"

That question caught my breath. I didn't respond right away, though I was surprised I had enough control over my ego to keep my mouth shut at that point. I was a know-it-all, after all. Instead, I took his question seriously and gave it some quiet thought.

What was I afraid of?

Deep down, I knew I wanted to be respected and recognized. I didn't want to lose that. And so, when my ego got triggered by something that could make me look bad, I got mean, disrespectful, and overly demanding.

Sitting in that chair, I thought about it more. It occurred to me that I had a great team: smart, talented, and responsive. I genuinely enjoyed the people I supported. There was sincere mutual respect. I loved the travel and interacting with different cultures. I wasn't worried that I would personally mess things up.

So why should I be afraid?

It hit me. I had my aha moment.

Finally, I said, "I don't have any reason to be afraid."

Don simply nodded, and that was that. Conversation over. He waved me out of his office so he could continue looking for whatever was in his desk drawer.

Don's work was done, but mine had just begun. Though I didn't have the name for it at the time, I had started to identify my first set of hidden metrics.

It's a long flight to Melbourne from Chicago, so I had plenty of time to sit quietly and examine my triggers, to understand them, and to get clear on how I wanted to act and how I wanted to be perceived at work. This is what I jotted down at the time: "Be fearless, and know, as a team, we can work through anything together," and "It's all about them, not me." This was the kickoff of my very first hidden metric.

There are personal and very private goals that we all create in our leadership journeys. Some of us notice and take seriously our "aha" moments—like I did—seeing them as opportunities to act and grow. Others may choose to see these moments as something to simply keep in the background.

Regardless of your personal choice here, you may not always want to share these new goals or intentions with others. It is perfectly permissible to keep them to yourself; to keep 'em hidden.

Why We Keep 'Em Hidden

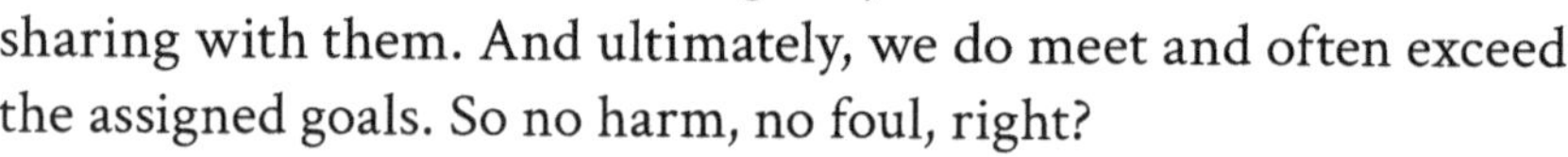

There are reasons why we keep these goals private. Some may say we coaches are not being honest with the sponsors of the coaching engagement. But I'd rather see to it as a sin of omission—something we just aren't sharing with them. And ultimately, we do meet and often exceed the assigned goals. So no harm, no foul, right?

Most coaching sponsors focus on leadership and team behaviors, such as delivering better presentations, improving relationships, strengthening team leadership, and developing more effective plans. Upon closer examination, these behaviors are somewhat vague and ambiguous.

Coaches know, though, that there is always, always something deeper getting in the way of achieving these fuzzy goals. It's that well-hidden stumbling block that I, as a coach, want to discover and help you overcome. While most coaches are not trained psychologists, we sometimes inadvertently help our clients uncover entrenched mindsets that hold them back.

So, I listen to the HRBP and my coachee's supervisor during the situational analysis meeting as they tell me what they want the coaching process to achieve. I write down the assigned goals, and I share them with my client. We both take them seriously, even though we will set them aside while we do the hidden work of coaching.

Most of my clients aren't interested in sharing these very personal and multifaceted goals with their bosses or HR reps. I am not either. I find it unnecessary. If we do share them, there is a chance they may be misinterpreted. Sponsors of coaching tend to seek out tangible, measurable behaviors, rather than the more personal mental and emotional shifts that often need to occur for meaningful growth to occur.

I've identified six ulterior motives for why my individual clients don't share their hidden metrics with anyone but their coach. See which of these resonates for you.

Why Hide 'Em #1: Fear of Asking for Help

My first book, *Mayday! Asking for Help in Times of Need,* explores reasons why we resist asking for help and how we can do it in a do-able, compassionate, self-respectful way. The reasons we hesitate to ask for help are all fear-based. Some won't ask for what they need because they don't want to be indebted to someone else (fear of surrendering to the cost of asking for help). Another won't ask because they are afraid of being seen as needy and no one will want to work with them (fear of separation from your team, group, or community). A third will hold back from asking for help because they are afraid of looking incompetent or weak or not a team player (fear of shame).

A common request for help that I often hear from newly promoted leaders is, "How can I possibly achieve my assigned goals if I am just listening to other more senior leaders talking in meeting after meeting?" They wonder, "What is the point of being in these meetings? What is my role as I listen? How do I define my new value-add? How can I be successful when I have received so little guidance? How do I stay motivated to do these new things?" It used to be so easy for them. "Just give me an assignment, and I'll get it done—with quality and on time," they would say. Unfortunately, those days disappeared with their old title.

If you have been given a new title, regardless of level, you may find yourself frustrated and confused as to how to hit your goals when you have no time to work on them. You will quickly discover that promotions demand you spend less time doing the work and more time sitting in meetings.

And damn, it is hard to ask for help on this particular topic.

If you, as a newly promoted manager, do ask for help, even from your supervisor, you may worry about what this says about your leadership abilities. No one, least of all you, wants to be seen as incompetent or out of the loop. Plus, no one wants to tell their boss that the new meetings are a time-suck. No one wants to suggest that listening to senior leaders is not the best use of their time. There is big fear that you'll come across as anything but a team player.

Now, my previously published book can help you figure out how to ask for help through curiosity, leadership, and ambition. That's easy. But more often, my coachees aren't ready to ask for help. I get that. It's not my job to push you to make those requests. I can challenge you to get out of your comfort zone and make the ask, but it is always up to you to decide what you will or will not do. If you say no, I will support you and your decision. In setting up hidden metrics, we focus on similar topics—not just the boring meetings, but also other sensitive topics. Not sharing these creates safety for you, as my client, while you find your footing.

Why Hide 'Em #2: Unhelpful Mindsets and Behaviors

Another reason we create hidden goals is that you may be holding on to beliefs and behaviors you wouldn't want anyone else to judge you for. It might be too easily misunderstood to disclose why you are working on these. Let me share an example.

A few years back, I coached Rajiv, born in India and now living in America. A brilliant marketing analyst, he was recently promoted to Senior VP from VP. His new supervisor invited Rajiv to every upcoming senior leadership team (SLT) meeting to discuss his team's research and data findings. These meetings would provide Rajiv with monthly opportunities to impress the SLT and to influence them as they made important decisions for the company. He was excited but worried too.

For months, his supervisor had been working to improve Rajiv's presentation skills. In preparation for each meeting, his boss would review the deck, edit it, and then tell Rajiv how to present. His advice went like this, "It's easy. Just look them all in the eyes." Or "You already know this stuff by heart, don't read the slides." Or, this gem, "Just imagine them all in their swimsuits!"

These review meetings got painful for Rajiv because, for some reason, he couldn't perform the way his boss wanted him to. As I pointed out earlier, adults rarely take advice. Rajiv was no different. Simply telling him to change his presentation style would never have succeeded. Something deeper was holding him back.

Through our coaching conversations, it became clear that Rajiv's home culture was deeply rooted in respect for hierarchy. As a result, his default behavior was to become modest and quiet in front of senior leaders. While there is nothing wrong with this perspective back in India, in his new work setting it was limiting him. No wonder Rajiv had a hard time speaking to those perched up higher on the career ladder. It was completely counter to how he was raised to view leadership in any organization.

So, together, he and I created a set of hidden metrics to help him shift away from his previous belief system to a new paradigm that was more empowering and energizing.

We didn't have to let anyone know we were working to update Rajiv's previous mindset. We kept it hush-hush, which gave Rajiv the space to reevaluate his perspective on the chain of command.

Over time, Rajiv began to see his leaders as partners rather than superiors. Not surprisingly, when this shift in perspective took hold, it automatically made Rajiv's presentation style more engaging, collaborative, and relaxed.

And bonus: working through his hidden metric allowed him to hit his assigned goal.

Why Hide 'Em #3: Long-Term Goals

The more senior you are in an organization, the more time-consuming and impactful your activities are. Experienced leaders frequently struggle with this. Your assigned goals may require months, even years, to complete, and they may touch thousands of lives both inside and outside the company.

For example, acquiring a new company and transitioning new staff can take months and require a whole new set of skills. How do you, as a leader with a impactful goals, stay focused, driven, and successful over that long stretch of time? How do you measure your progress when it feels like it's going to take forever to make it happen?

Through hidden metrics, of course. Coaches often work with seasoned leaders to find uniquely personal approaches to stay inspired over long periods. As the person in charge, you must learn to celebrate your own meaningful points of progress because they won't be obvious to others. Finding ongoing satisfaction and positive momentum won't be as easy as it used to be, since the tasks are so enormous and often quite nebulous. It may be months before you can check off items on your trusty to-do list.

If this is your situation, you and I will create daily, weekly, and monthly goals and measures—aligned with your values and strengths—to keep you stimulated and enthusiastic over the long months and years.

Margie had this experience. As head of HR for her employer's European region, Margie was tasked with completely updating and revising the HR operating model across nine countries. She estimated it would take three years to successfully complete this objective. This enormous challenge required her to stay motivated for at least thirty-six months, if not longer. It was a daunting plan, and Margie was determined to succeed.

Together, Margie and I focused on keeping her eye on her assigned business goals and finding and celebrating small wins based on what mattered to her. For Margie, this meant listening beyond the facts, hearing people's stories, connecting with them, and being of service to them when she could. For example, she began to count the personal wins that had occurred during the one-on-ones she held with her direct reports. Each week, she tracked her successes (the ones that were personally meaningful) and lessons learned, including what to do differently next time. Each month, she measured how much closer she was to becoming the leader she aspired to be.

Margie's supervisors in HR and the European region were clear about her assigned goals, but they would not have had the time or interest in learning what would motivate her. So, we kept that hidden.

Why Hide 'Em #4: Confidential Feelings

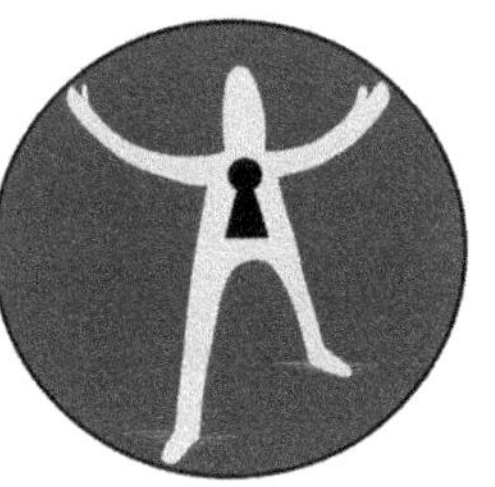

There are risks to new and experienced leaders alike in sharing with others when you feel demotivated, disengaged, or discouraged at work. Working with a coach, you can develop hidden metrics to reinvigorate your leadership in these situations too.

Will was a seasoned and trusted leader. Despite all his obvious success, he was feeling uninspired. Once Will understood the confidential nature of our coaching relationship, he readily shared with me everything he was feeling. He divulged he was bored out of his mind sitting in meeting after meeting (not surprising). Additionally, because his team consistently delivered high-quality work, he didn't feel he had much to contribute. His day-to-day felt blah.

Will would have been at risk telling his supervisor that he didn't care about his job anymore—that is not the kind of message any boss wants to hear. So, Will and I created hidden metrics to track his personal progress. As we began our coaching engagement, we added hidden goals and metrics to his list of assigned business goals.

Together, we had conversations about what would get Will back on track. We devised metrics that challenged him to get more out of his work by deepening his relationships with peers and supervisors, asking new kinds of questions in meetings, and interacting with his team using a coaching mindset. It worked. Will got out of his rut by simply focusing on what had real meaning for him.

Why Hide 'Em #5: Audacious Goals

Sometimes the goals a coaching client comes up with are simply beyond what anyone else thinks is possible. You may have a new product that no one has thought of before. Or perhaps you know in your gut you belong in the C-suite, but no one yet sees you as a senior leader.

Theses audacious goals are born from your intuition. They represent your values and aspirations for a better future.

Risk arises when you share your bold idea with someone else. The idea may be dismissed out of hand as not feasible. Or someone may steal your idea or act on it before you have a chance to.

If you share too early, the idea may not be fully formed yet. To achieve your vision, it needs to be supported and nurtured by facts, data, and an initial plan. Sometimes, it's best to keep these ideas under wraps until you're truly prepared to share them.

But you can share them with your coach. Your coach will keep your audacious idea secret and offer up as much tender, loving care for your idea as they can.

Later in Chapter 4, I have a great, real-life example of a leader who was forced to keep his bold goals a secret. Hang in there. It's a great story!

Why Hide 'Em #6: Feedback Isn't Relevant or Accurate

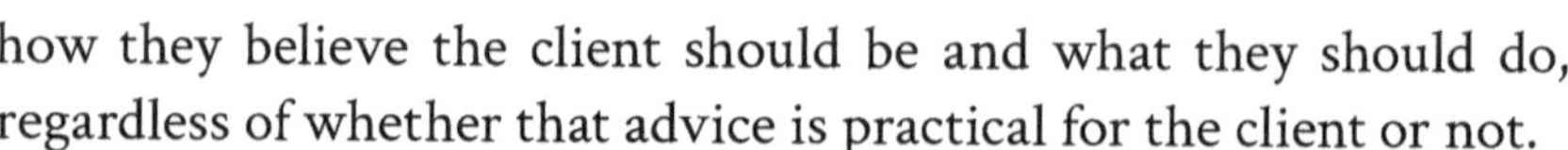

The final reason we keep these metrics secret is that supervisors may give feedback that is either irrelevant or inaccurate. This tends to happen when a supervisor projects onto my client how they believe the client should be and what they should do, regardless of whether that advice is practical for the client or not.

Perhaps you've received feedback that doesn't sit right with you. Maybe you and your supervisor have different styles, and they want you to be more like them. Let's say you've received the feedback without defensiveness, but you can't see yourself behaving the way they want you to. Besides, you like how you are. Perhaps they are slower and more methodical in their work style and you are quicker and strategic. What do you do with their feedback when you know it would not be authentic for you to try to be like them?

Sometimes the advice you've been given is antiquated in two ways. First, it may be based on behaviors you exhibited in the past, though not currently. Second, the advice or feedback may come from outdated leadership models that are no longer acceptable. For example, women and people of color still get feedback about how they need to behave, dress, or talk to fit in. This discriminatory messaging runs counter to current management thought about authenticity and diversity.

Working with your coach, you'll find a way to determine what it is your boss ultimately wants from you. Perhaps it's more about reviewing your work or involving others in the discussion (rather than rushing through) and taking it one step at a time. Your coach can help you create hidden metrics that give your boss what they need in a way that works for you. And they don't need to know about it.

There may be more reasons to keep your hidden metrics invisible, but these are the ones I see most frequently. Just remember: You don't have to share your hidden metrics with anyone unless you want to. It is entirely up to you to decide.

The Psychology of Metrics

For centuries, the business world has been obsessed with measuring everything that contributes or detracts from overall efficiency. Greater efficiency equals more dollars. In the late 1800s, time and motion studies were introduced.

Consultants back then were highly interested in improving efficiencies by analyzing how much time a task took, as well as the physical movements of those tasks. The purpose was to streamline workflows, eliminate unnecessary actions, and establish standards for task completion times. Those implementing time and motion studies tended to view the people doing the work as cogs in a machine, rather than as real people. There's still some of that around. Amazon and Walmart both have these kinds of standards established to speed up their distribution systems.

The mid-twentieth century brought us management by objectives (MBO). Later came key performance indicators (KPIs) and SMART goals (specific, measurable, achievable, relevant and time-bound).

Companies still use traditional metrics to:

- ✔ Hit or exceed monetary goals.
- ✔ Help senior leaders get a sense of progress or regression.
- ✔ Provide a sense of security that the company or team is on the right track and can course-correct, if needed.
- ✔ Give leadership a sense of clarity and order.
- ✔ Motivate individuals and teams, helping them see who is in first place.
- ✔ Create reward or punishment systems.

Each evolution in measurements made us better at tracking progress toward financial goals. But they all shared one critical blind spot: They couldn't measure what matters most to the people doing the work.

Typically, for a metric to be effective, it must measure something observable, such as a home run, a sale, or a faster turnaround. Most bosses want to see progress before they believe it has happened. For example, a boss prefers to see you, with their own eyes, interacting more collaboratively with your counterparts, not just hearing you tell them this is now a priority. Essentially, if your supervisor doesn't observe it firsthand or hear about your behavior changes from a trusted source, they likely won't believe the change has taken place. Think of it this way: in this age of smart phones, if you haven't snapped a picture of you with the celebrity, it didn't really happen. Your supervisor wants to see the evidence.

Unfortunately, because upper management is focused on the big behavior changes, they may miss the potent but quieter shifts in actions, emotions, and mindsets.

Observable Change

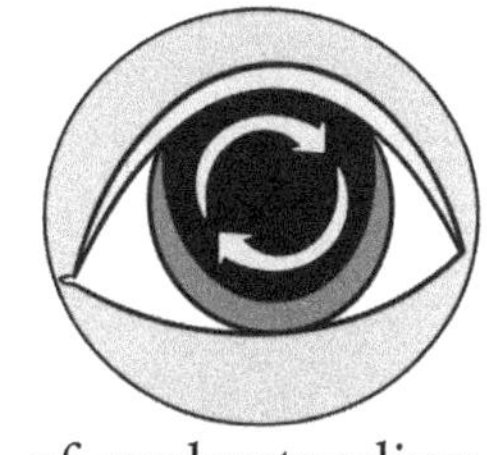

In coaching, we look for both big and small observable changes. Sometimes, behavior shifts are so subtle and fleeting that it's hard to see them. Often, these observable behaviors are as simple as a nod of the head or a soft smile of understanding. Coaches are trained to identify these shifts in your emotions, mindsets, and actions.

Coaches will notice how your speech patterns may incorporate more optimistic vocabulary, which may make you sound more like a leader. We detect emotional shifts, such as when you move from uncertainty to confidence, i.e., "I think I can" to "I know I can!" And we discern when you experience a paradigm shift, like Rajiv did when he began to see his superiors as colleagues.

Here's an example. Professional coaches don't get certified unless their coaching is assessed and observed by other more experienced and qualified coaches. When I was taking my final coaching exam to become a certified coach, I had to coach someone in front of a group of other experienced coaches. At one point, I asked a question of my client that profoundly shifted him. I don't remember the details, but I remember his eyes welled up with tears, and he nodded agreement to my question rather than using his voice. He couldn't speak at that point; he was too choked up.

The fact is, I *saw* him experience this shift. But one observing coach didn't catch it. She gave me feedback that I had missed an opportunity with him, but I hadn't. She was facing me, not my client. She couldn't see his reaction. Thankfully, the other experienced coaches had witnessed what my coaching question had prompted.

That's when a key lesson landed on me. Sometimes, the progress we make is restrained and subtle. Your supervisor may completely miss a behavior change that you worked hard to adopt. However, your trained coach will be looking for these imperceptible behavior shifts. When they see one, they'll acknowledge it and celebrate your growth, which provides you with the feedback and energy to continue with the vital work you're doing.

Coaches also seek out the more obvious, apparent changes in behavior. That's why we ask you to report back on what you're doing differently and better and why we often touch base with your colleagues to see how things are progressing.

However, even significant and noticeable changes may not be apparent right away. Remember my toxic behavior? I was determined to transform my unprofessional conduct. Unfortunately, my old reputation followed me for a long time. Co-workers did not always notice my version 2.0. If they did, they may have assumed it was just a temporary thing. It's also hard to prove a negative—to show I'm not doing something. But that shift in me was more or less permanent. I give myself a 9 out of 10 knowing that every once in a decade I can revert to old behaviors. Even now, current colleagues are surprised when I tell them how toxic I used to be.

My supervisor Don and I both ended up leaving the company after a year or so. Later, we met for lunch, and he commented on how much I had changed, for the better. It's still the best feedback I have ever received!

Ultimately, it doesn't matter if others witnessed my growth. I know I changed. I am proud of myself for being able to shift away from fear and embrace trust with my team. You, too, will experience a similar sense of pride and accomplishment when you achieve your own hidden metrics.

Life School

In those early years of my career, I only saw half the picture. I was more focused on hitting my assigned goals, which I thought were of utmost importance. After all, that's what I was getting paid to do.

When we focus solely on achieving what has been delegated to us, we lose out on a great deal of personal growth. We miss the opportunity to strengthen ourselves and to embolden others, too. We fail at what one of my teachers calls "Life School," the lessons that come to us, whether through work or home, that make us better humans.

The traditional metrics we are given at work don't begin to touch on the messy and weighty lessons we acquire daily. They are inadequate, unable to capture what it means to be a human being, as we learn many of our lessons while at work.

Hidden metrics, on the other hand, represent your own Life School lessons. To be successful, Rajiv had to recognize how he was getting in his own way and accept the personal life lesson that he was playing small in corporate America. To succeed, he had to reframe his relationship to himself, as well as to his colleagues.

In the same way, Margie had to identify what inspired her on a regular basis and keep those things front and center, even in the face of a long and drawn-out project. She couldn't allow herself to focus only on the problems, issues, and challenges. She had to be deliberate and search for the silver lining and small moments of joy every day. That's not easy for most of us to do. Over time, Margie became known for her positive take, and her optimism became contagious.

I had my life lessons, too. I had to raise my awareness of when I was afraid, explore the fear, and actively set it aside.

Some days, while I am waiting for my next in-person client to arrive, I look out onto the sea of office buildings around me and think about how each window in each building represents at least one person—and in downtown Chicago there are tens of thousands of windows. I think about how each soul in each window is going through their own Life School. I'd love to ask each one, "What is your job teaching you today?"

More Than Meets the Eye

One way to think of your hidden metrics is as the invisible mental and emotional labor required to achieve success that matters to you.

Consider the unseen and underappreciated work that women have long carried out in managing households. *Mental load*—we now have a term for it—is the invisible head and heart labor that occurs in managing the details for the family: scheduling and remembering dentist appointments, tracking grocery lists, packing and planning activities for family vacations, coordinating family schedules. The list is practically endless.

Women tend to bear the weight of these responsibilities without anyone noticing or compensating them for it. Just because no one recognizes the invisible labor doesn't mean it doesn't exist. It very much does.

Mental load activities are often unending. Think about it. The laundry must be done and meals planned—every day of the week, every week of the month, and every month of the year—in perpetuity. Even when the entire family is on vacation, tasks still need to be anticipated and completed. Just remembering it all can be exhausting.

The significant distinction between mental load and hidden metrics is that hidden metrics are energy-producing, not energy-draining. Once you start moving toward your secret goals, you will feel more energy with each new accomplishment. This, in turn, will compel you to take another step forward.

Advanced Human Skill Sets

Hidden metrics, in another way, capture the skills, behaviors, and mindsets that some may categorize as "soft skills." While they may be harder to measure because they are not as easily observed, there's nothing soft about maintaining professional relationships, inspiring teams, or navigating complex human dynamics. These are advanced human skills that require tremendous emotional intelligence and practice.

Look at any major corporate failure and you'll rarely find technical incompetence at its root. Instead, you'll find leaders who couldn't build trust, teams that couldn't communicate effectively, and cultures that valued profits over people. You will also see leaders who got sidetracked and focused solely on the bottom line, rather than values, strengths, and an inspiring purpose.

I'm talking about companies like Boeing, which used to be known as a leader in building innovative airliners but is now seen as frighteningly lacking in quality. The company's vision shifted from doing the right thing to doing the expedient thing. New senior leaders became notorious for failing to communicate effectively with their engineers, compliance experts, and quality specialists. Multiple whistleblowers demonstrated that Boeing had prioritized shareholder value over respect and quality.

And, if I'm being honest, this was my problem early in my career. I was so caught up in hitting my targets that I didn't care about how I treated people.

Now, I know better.

Hidden metrics create clear pathways toward something more meaningful than the bottom line: your values, strengths, and driving purpose. They may require you to listen differently, to think strategically, or to speak tactfully. But as you watch yourself move closer to becoming the brilliant leader you suspect you can be, these skill sets will go on to inspire you and the people you lead.

The Four Cornerstones of Meaning

Hidden metrics are robust precisely because they're personally meaningful to you, not your supervisor, not your peers and not your squad. They matter to you alone.

But do you know what is meaningful to you?

Meaning itself is a question for philosophers, but we can grapple with it in a simplified, more practical way. For our purposes, let's define meaning as something of individualized and personal significance to you.

AMeaningOfLife.org, an insightful online resource from Randall Grayson, PhD, categorizes Four Cornerstones of Meaning that can help you define what is most meaningful to you.

1. **Love:** The strongest of the Four Cornerstones, love refers to how you relate to people, yourself, and others.

   While we don't often use the word "love" at work, we do build tight relationships that can last a lifetime. Frequently, we do deeply care about the people we work with. So, to determine how to find meaning in relating to others and yourself, ask yourself these questions: How do I see myself at work? Am I as authentic as I want to be? Am I trustworthy? Am I trusting? How well do I respect myself by upholding my own personal values? Do I consistently demonstrate kindness and empathy in my daily interactions? Who do I care for at work and why? What if my personal connections at work disappeared? How would I feel? What would I miss?

2. **Expression:** Refers to art, music, poetry, writing for some, and storytelling for all. 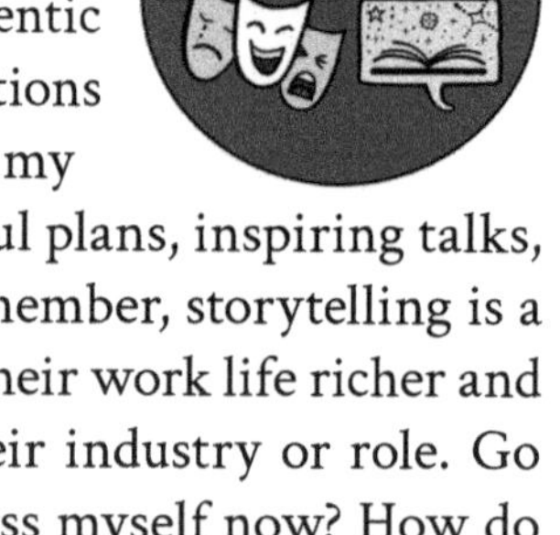

   Ask yourself: How do I express my authentic self at work? Do I? In what kinds of situations or meetings? How do I allow myself and my voice to show up? Is it through thoughtful plans, inspiring talks, or sharing my wisdom with others? Remember, storytelling is a skill that everyone can employ to make their work life richer and create a bigger impact, regardless of their industry or role. Go deeper and ask yourself: How do I express myself now? How do I want to convey my true essence? How would I feel if I were no longer able to voice my opinions or share experiences?

3. **Discovery and Exploration:** Concerns the discovery and exploration of you, yourself.
   Consider how open you are to learning about your strengths and weaknesses. Ask yourself: How do I find meaning in my personal growth and becoming more of who I am? Am I willing to confront my triggers and fears? Am I willing to risk something new that might make me a tad nervous? How can I challenge myself to be more and do more? What if I were no longer encouraged to do and be more? How would that affect me emotionally and professionally?

4. **Service:** Addresses the meaning you experience when you give to something outside of yourself.
   At work, your job, ultimately, is to give of

yourself, to be of service to those you lead, and to support your peers and upper leadership. So ask yourself: How am I doing this now? How can I be of more service to those around me? What particular need calls to me and my specific set of skills and talents? How can I help best? What if no one needed what I had to offer? How would that make me feel?

Spending time contemplating these Four Cornerstones of Meaning can help you pinpoint those things that are of consequence to you. Later, in the Workbook section, you'll have space to jot down your thoughts and insights.

Let's revisit the hidden vision I created way back when, from my era of high bangs and masculine suits. I didn't let anyone know I was working on new goals for myself. I kept them invisible. And while management might have advised me to "become more collaborative in working with others," my true goal was to learn to manage my fear and to trust in the capabilities of the people around me. While this was generally a good thing for me to accomplish and beneficial for the company, what kept me inspired was the meaning I found in the journey.

I found a great deal of meaning in personal self-discovery as I explored my fears and learned how to manage them. I also found greater satisfaction in serving my team by focusing on their development, not just their work product. I created a better relationship with myself and my colleagues, including the shared services team, who had previously called me out on my bad behavior. It mattered to me that I repair those relationships. The meaning I found may not have been relevant to anyone else, but it was profoundly important to me. I look back now and see it as a time of rapid and insightful learning at Life School.

Believe me when I say: the most important measurements in your career will never appear on a spreadsheet. They're the moments when you choose patience over pressure, empathy over efficiency, and growth over immediate gains.

The Coach's Secret

Professional coaches recognize the power in hidden metrics. The formidable combination of confidentiality, personal meaning, and the use of measures to track progress is fundamental to the success of any coaching engagement.

On your own or working with a coach, you will find yourself setting secret goals too. You'll learn why the most powerful changes often happen beneath the surface and how to harness these concealed forces to transform your leadership.

Because, in the end, your legacy won't be measured in quarterly reports or annual reviews. It will be calculated in the lives you've influenced, the teams you've built, and the culture you've created. And, in the deep satisfaction you carry in your heart.

But first, you're going to want to let go of some things.

2
HIDDEN EXPECTATIONS

Before we delve into the details of creating your hidden metrics, let's take a closer look at the transition that occurs when you are promoted, whether for the first or fifth time.

Meet my former client Chris, who, over a few short years, had proved himself to be a highly capable individual contributor. Chris was the "get it done" guy, no matter what "it" was. Clear-thinking, smart, tactical, and direct, Chris had also earned his MBA while working full-time. I was brought in to coach him soon after his promotion to help him become the leader everyone assumed he could be. Like many others, Chris was promoted based on his performance as a doer rather than as a leader of people. Because he had demonstrated that he was the person who could accomplish the impossible, senior leadership thought it was time to give him his own team.

While Chris quite liked the idea of being a team lead, he wasn't quite sure how his new role would be different from his old one. To gain a little clarity, I asked to speak with his team of direct reports, and he agreed. In my conversation with them, his team shared that he was too "in the weeds." Chris didn't know how to step back and let them do the work.

In other words, Chris didn't know how to let go of his past role of being a doer.

In our coaching conversations, Chris admitted that he genuinely missed doing the work and chafed at sitting in endless meetings. He suspected he was focusing on the wrong things, but as a team leader, he figured his job was to help his team. So, despite his better judgment, he allowed himself to get too involved, to control decision-making, and to continue being the expert. Fortunately, Chris's team was more than capable of achieving their goals without his hovering and expertise. With coaching, Chris realized he was hindering, not assisting. He was killing their confidence by always having the answer and micromanaging their decisions.

I felt empathy for his squad. We've all worked with micro-managers. We know how demoralizing it can be to have every word scrutinized and every decision questioned. Having your leader sit next to you checking on your work in real-time is a confidence killer.

Chris was also spending too much time verifying his team's deliverables, which left him unable to focus on what he should have been doing as their boss and as a member of his new peer team. He wasn't working on a vision, creating development plans, or looking for ways to support his new supervisor.

How many times do you see this? Strong players moved into positions for which they are ill-trained. Most companies don't have the resources to hire an experienced leader, so they ask the best player to step up. Chris was thrown into a role he wasn't prepared for. And he longed for what he used to do, how he used to contribute. For him, his past role had been clear. Now, poor Chris wasn't the least bit certain as to what, exactly, he should be doing with his time.

Had there been a stronger support system for Chris, he may have learned about the natural changes that happen when you get promoted. But he didn't, so he had to discover them the hard way.

What No One Tells You: Hidden Expectations

When you finally get the nod, the new title, and the new office, the feeling of pride and accomplishment is exciting but short-lived. It is soon replaced by new challenges that no one bothered to warn you about. These natural shifts surface when we move from doing to leading. Each shift requires us to let go of our past and what we did before the promotion and to embrace new mindsets and ways of being and doing. Many hidden metrics emerge because of these shifts.

What exactly changes when we move from doing to leading? I've captured fifteen adjustments to anticipate. Whether you choose to implement these shifts or not, it is likely your colleagues will still expect you to.

Shift #1: From Nothing Has Changed to Everything Has Changed

Just because you feel like you are the same person you have always been, despite the promotion, please understand that is not how others see you. You are now viewed through the lens of what your title and office represent. Your former peers may begin to interact with you differently, and certainly, your new peer group and boss will treat you differently as well.

Let go of: Your old vision of yourself.

That old vision of yourself no longer aligns with how others see you. It's time to accept that there's a cost to each promotion, and that means you may have to start seeing yourself differently, just like they do.

Instead, embrace: Yourself as a leader.

✓ Own your new role. Learn to accept that how others perceive you will be through your title. When you catch yourself saying, "But I haven't changed . . ." stop yourself and remember that you will have to change—grow—to succeed.

✓ Get clear on the kind of leader you want to be and give yourself permission to be that leader. Get a sense of your current reputation by asking trusted co-workers. Then decide if that reputation is adequate for the legacy you want to leave. If not, consider the reputation you want to have and begin building toward it. Take the time to observe others in your peer group. Learn what is considered appropriate behavior on your new team. Begin to adopt those actions that will elevate your leadership.

Shift #2: From "Your" Team to a New Team

You have a new team now. The friendships you had with your direct reports must change.

Let go of: Being friends with your old squad.

Your friendships with your former team will always be meaningful; those folks might even be after-work buddies. However, if you've been promoted, you will be expected to establish clear boundaries with them. As much as you'd like to keep things the same, hanging out with your former peers or your new squad invites risk and threatens your reputation and your effectiveness. Indeed, others may view you as playing favorites or being too close to be objective.

Instead, embrace: You are a member of a new team.

✓ Think of your direct reports and skip-levels, if you have them, as your second team or squad. See yourself, in relation to them, as separate. Every professional sport has teams led by coaches or managers. Phil Jackson, retired coach of the Chicago Bulls, was not a peer of Michael Jordan or Scottie Pippen. His role was to lead, not play. Same for you: Lead or lead not. (How did Yoda get in here?)

✓ Your new team deserves your attention. This shift in perspective will impact how you support each other. For example, if you receive unflattering feedback about something your squad did or didn't do, pause before you jump to a knee-jerk defense of them. Instead, consider how your peers and their direct reports are affected by your squad's actions.

✓ Your most important relationship from now on is between you and your supervisor. Your ability to connect, build trust, and be vulnerable with your boss has a direct impact on your long-term success as a professional, and on your ability to create a meaningful career. Learn who they are, how they got where they are, how they prefer to lead, along with what is important to them. Become a supportive business partner to them and learn how to anticipate their needs.

✓ Upper management now expects you to be rigorous in maintaining strong boundaries between you and your team. You'll be expected to hold on to confidential information.

✓ Give credit to your peers and their directs. When you notice them do something great, tell them. You do this for your squad, so spread the love. Let your peers know they are seen and recognized for their good work. Show your appreciation.

Shift #3: From Tasks to Relationships

A worker's value is found in their ability to achieve the goals that have been set. A leader's value resides in their ability to get things done through others. This requires you to be able to create, repair, and maintain relationships, as well as inspire those around you.

Let go of: The belief that work is all about being in the action.

Focus less on doing the work or being the expert. This also applies to doing too much work. Being super busy doesn't necessarily get you the recognition you want. It can convey an inability to set boundaries or priorities. That old paradigm will eventually hold you back as a leader.

Instead, embrace: Building quality relationships.

✔ Examine the relationships you have with your peers and superiors at work. Determine which ones need more attention. Request fifteen to thirty minutes to meet with your skip-level supervisors to learn their stories and find out what is most important to them and their teams. (Leaders love that.) Build new relationships with them, one cup of coffee at a time, and find out what you have in common: families, hobbies, films, etc.

✔ Create and nurture these new relationships; a consistent connection leads to better work products, increased collaboration, and greater influence. After your initial meeting, be sure to check in periodically. Send articles or social media posts that may be relevant to your previous conversations.

✔ Recognize the value of these new connections. As you rise in your organization, your comfort with these people will pay off. Long-lasting, trusting business relationships make higher-level decision-making easier. Over time, because you have invested in these relationships, they will have learned to trust you. They will cut you some slack when you make an error or when you suggest something new and unusual.

✔ If you have new direct reports, now is an ideal time to get to know them. Not just their titles, work histories, or strengths—ask them questions about what they enjoy at work. What makes for an excellent day for them? What do they need more of at work? What kind of accolades do they prefer (some want open praise, others prefer a simple "great job")? Ask how you can best assist them.

✔ If you are now leading a team of people who used to be your peers, this is also a great opportunity to get to know them in a different way. You may think you know them now, but there is always more to learn about a person. Think of it this way: What you have is a map of a colleague, but this map is missing lots of other significant features. Part of your new job as their leader is to ask them different questions so you can fill in the missing parts of the existing map. Plus, these former peers are now going to be knocking on your office door to talk about things they might never have shared with you before, like struggles, fears, challenges, and aspirations.

✔ Create effective one-on-ones. Ask your directs to bring more than status reports to these meetings. Have them share their successes and challenges. Talk to them about what it means to be a leader. Get them to define their own leadership style. Share books or articles you've read about leadership and ask them to do the same. Brainstorm with them on how to improve the team. Use this valuable time to grow your leaders.

Shift #4: From Being Developed to Developing Others

It is now your responsibility to develop your squad. Be on the lookout for new training and on-the-job opportunities to help them grow. Challenge them to perform beyond their current levels. Be deliberate in helping them achieve their career goals.

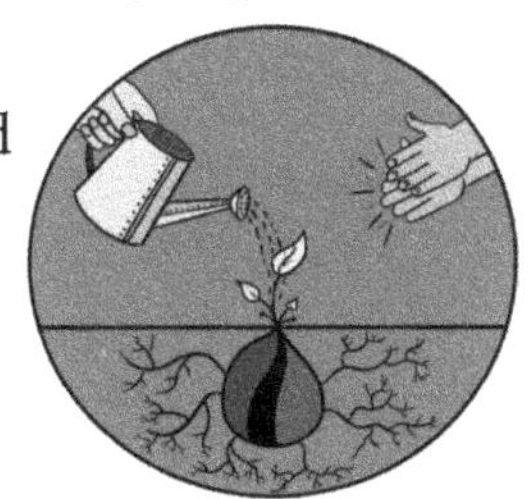

Let go of: Focusing only on your own professional development.

Your squad is now counting on you to develop them and their capabilities.

Instead, embrace: Celebrating others' growth.

✔ Create development plans for each person reporting to you. Set goals, identify potential action steps, and schedule a completion date. At a minimum, revisit this every quarter and check progress.

✔ Look for on-the-job opportunities to develop your people. Delegate not just what they could do but what you want them to learn to do. Yes, delegation removes tasks from your to-do list, but it is primarily an approach to develop the skills of others.

✔ When someone does well, acknowledge them and celebrate a job well done. Make your recognition sincere. Acknowledge the cost of the achievement or its value to the company. For example, "Thanks for getting that deck to me on time. I know you had to re-prioritize some things and work late. I appreciate what you did. It will help us clarify our vision for senior leadership."

✔ Pay attention to your team members when they apply their strengths, such as listening or creating work plans. Notice how their levels of satisfaction and fulfillment rise when they do what feels right to them.

✔ Work with your HR representative to identify external training or coaching options to develop your team members.

✔ Let go of being the primary decision-maker for your team. Encourage your directs to make decisions and live with the benefits and consequences of them.

✔ Step away from being the voice of the team. Allow your trusted directs to represent the team. Give them a chance to shine in front of others.

Shift #5: Shifting from Motivation to Inspiration

Though we often use these concepts interchangeably, there is a difference. *Motivation* comes from an external source, like a boss telling you what to do. Naturally, as good employees, we are motivated to do what they ask of us. On the other hand, *inspiration* comes from something internal—a unique spark that compels us to create and move forward. The word itself means to "breathe into." Generally, we motivate others by giving them clear tasks to complete. But we inspire ourselves—and others—with exciting visions of what is possible.

Let go of: Telling people what to do.

In your new role, you are expected to motivate your squad with clear directions. That's what a manager does: They manage the work. As a leader, you are expected to inspire your people not just to complete the job but to go above and beyond.

Instead, embrace: Inspiring others.

✔ Figure out what inspires you first. What is a great day for you? What did you get to do? What satisfied you? What helped you maintain the momentum? What made you want to do more? Remember the Four Cornerstones of Meaning? Meaning inspires.

✔ Now learn what excites the others you work with. What do they find meaningful? These are the things that get us in the zone, the groove, the flow.

✔ Take a step back and look for common points of meaning. Incorporate these elements into your language, presentations, and conversations. Reinforce them as often as possible. Remind everyone that this is what keeps them engaged and inspired.

✔ Look for what each person does well—their strengths. Those are naturally energizing. Seek opportunities to let them apply those strengths. Avoid focusing on what they don't do well. That is, frankly, a downer. I'll cover more about strengths in Chapter 7.

✔ Your value as a leader lies in getting things done through others, not doing them yourself. It's easier if you know what will inspire them to do the work.

Shift #6: From Actions to Emotions

One of the hardest things to accept when moving from doing to leading is how much time you will spend with emotions (Gasp! Yes, emotions—at work.) Those who follow your lead will look to you to be a sounding board and a shoulder to cry on. In private one-on-ones, you will inevitably hear about challenges and struggles, and you'll be expected to hold these in confidence.

Let go of: Old mindsets about emotions.

Think back to a time you confided in your boss. Now, multiply that by the number of direct reports you have. That's a lot of emotions. Your new job is not just to ensure the work gets done, but also to provide the support needed for the people doing the work. That often means dealing with feelings and highly emotional situations. Once you become a leader, it becomes less about you and more about them.

Instead, embrace: The power of emotions.

✔ Each emotion has a story to tell and serves as a driver of action. Someone feeling indignant has a story that someone has impinged on their reputation or dignity. Indignation prompts us to speak up, clear the air, and set the record straight. Understanding the emotions someone is expressing helps you empathize and discern what questions to ask. A helpful resource for introducing you to the stories and actions prompted by emotions is *The Field Guide to Emotions* by Curtis Watkins and Dan Newby.

✔ Emotions cannot be erased from the workplace nor can they be erased from the worker for that matter. Emotions are always present for everyone. Become aware of how emotions float under the surface of and support your conversations, and you'll quickly discern the meaningful undercurrents. I've had a few clients who have been told they are unemotional. That's not true. These clients experience big feelings just like everyone else; they may simply not share them openly. When they do, it's essential to listen carefully.

✔ The most profound impact you can have on your squad comes from being fully present with them and listening completely. Listening includes not only hearing the words but also noticing the emotions that are often conveyed through body language. Set aside distractions and focus on the human being sitting in front of you.

✔ When someone shares something personal and emotional outside the realm of work, like a cancer diagnosis or the death of a loved one, acknowledge what they are experiencing. Demonstrate that you have heard them. "Oh, that's awful news. I'm so sorry. That must be difficult for you and your family right now." Then, listen some more. Avoid shifting the conversation to focus on you and your experiences. Give them time to talk first.

Shift #7: From Tactical to Strategic

One of the toughest transitions new leaders must make is to stop thinking about what needs to be done today or this week. Instead, a leader must learn to see projects and challenges with a strategic eye, understanding how the work your team produces fits into the whole and how the enterprise fits into the market. Considering and exploring the long-term impact of decisions and actions is exactly what we rely on our leaders to do.

Let go of: The day-to-day tasks.

No one really wants you to do the "work" anymore. Not your boss and not your squad. Resist hovering.

Instead, embrace: A strategic mindset.

✔ Set your attention on the big picture and long-term vision for your squad and the company. Ask yourself: How could your functional squad be operating a year from now? What would success look like then? What resources, skills, and competencies would your squad need then? How would your accomplishments help your peers and your company's performance?

✔ Set aside time to think. Yes, think. As challenging as it will be to block off time on your calendar, get into the practice now. Resist the temptation to focus solely on what you and your squad need to succeed. Figure out what you, your directs, your peers, and your supervisor need. See the tapestry, not just the stitches.

✔ Take a good look at your processes and systems. What processes are slow and clunky? What can be automated? How can you use AI to speed things up? Assign trusted directs to implement these improvements. These opportunities will also teach them to be more strategically minded.

✔ Trust your squad to do what they've been trained to do. We easily trust others who are competent, reliable, and authentic. Determine if your direct reports are competent; if not, uptrain them so they are. Are they reliable? Do they show up and deliver when promised? If not, figure out what is getting in their way. And then, step back. Let them know you are available to assist and answer questions but avoid doing the work for them. Allow them a chance to prove themselves. I've included a whole section on trust in Chapter 9.

✔ Learn to delegate as much as you can. The one thing that trips up my clients when they are delegating is agreeing on how progress is to be communicated. Are you following up to check on the status, or will your direct report be responsible for that? (I recommend the latter.) What if your direct report gets stuck? When should they come to you for assistance? And how will you know the work is completed and to your standards? Agree early on how you will communicate with each other. Remember to acknowledge them when they succeed.

Shift #8: From Passive to Active in Meetings

The number one complaint I hear from coachees is how frustrated they feel as they sit for hours on end in meeting after meeting. "The 'work' is back at my desk," they whine. These new and experienced leaders alike miss the point. Actively absorbing the shared information, varying perspectives, interpersonal dynamics, and demonstrated leadership IS your work now.

Let go of: Old mindsets about the value of meetings.

While your supervisor may still want you to do some of the work and handle leading your squad, it's more important than ever for you to be fully present in leadership meetings. How you spend your time in these meetings will have a considerable impact on your future.

Instead, embrace: Being a full participant in meetings.

✔ Consider yourself lucky to be part of these meetings. This is where proprietary information is discussed. At a minimum, you will learn about market standing, vision, direction, organizational changes—all the great inside scoop. Use this information wisely.

✔ Attending these meetings also provides a comprehensive view into the interpersonal and leadership dynamics of those on your new team. Observe and learn how each player attempts to influence and how conflicts are (or are not) addressed.

✔ As you listen to what is discussed, consider not only how this impacts you and your team, but also how it affects other departments.

✔ Determine who senior leadership pays most attention to. What is it about their language and mindsets that appeals to leadership? Is it fact-based or simply passionate? Do these parties already have a close relationship, or are they still getting to know each other?

✔ How does trust show up, or not, in these meetings? Chapter 9 will help you answer this question.

Shift #9: From Doing to Thinking

As a doer of work, your to-do list drives your days. As a leader, however, your to-do list becomes much smaller, with fewer larger tasks. Depending on the scope of your responsibilities, your to-do list may even become non-existent. Instead, your time will be marked by meetings, conversations, and strategic reflection.

Let go of: Doing the work.

At the risk of repeating myself, your value as a leader is very different from your value as a doer. With your promotion, your supervisor will expect you to spend less time performing and more time thinking, strategizing, anticipating, and planning. You will be expected to get things done through others, rather than doing them yourself.

Instead, embrace: Your experience and knowledge.

✓ Learn to trust your experience and knowledge. You may not know everything, but you do have a specific set of capabilities to draw from. If ideas surface and you aren't sure they will fly, socialize them with trusted colleagues first before formally proposing them.

✓ You will find yourself in situations where you don't have the "answer" readily at hand. Learn to trust your years of experience and your intuition. Over time, you will become less of an expert. Instead, you will become wiser. Learn to rely on your wisdom.

✓ Nothing in nature stays the same; everything changes. With organizations, you can choose how these changes happen. Ask yourself, "What would an ideal change look like? How can we make that happen?"

✓ If you have more of an analytical mind, meaning you appreciate data, logic, and process, you can challenge yourself to move beyond your comfort zone. How much data do you require to make an informed decision? Probably not as much as you think. Do your research, yes, but avoid the dreaded analysis paralysis.

✔ As mentioned before, set aside time to think. You won't need days, but you might need an hour here or there every few weeks to step back and assess everything. Be rigorous with your calendar and book that time just for thinking.

Shift #10: From Yes to No

We all like to say yes to new opportunities, but moving up in an organization means understanding when to say no. Taking on too much and always being there for others can work against you. Taking on too many special projects can distract you from your leadership role.

Let go of: Being the hero.

Who doesn't like being relied upon to solve problems or give the right answer? When we save the day, our feelings of self-worth and confidence skyrocket. However, in your new role it is time to encourage your squad to solve the problems. That way you can stay focused on being a leader, not a hero.

Instead, embrace: Protecting your time.

✔ Set your priorities. Identify what is most important, even if everything seems a top priority. If helpful, share your priorities with your supervisor. Get them to agree to this list of key initiatives. Do this periodically to ensure you are always in alignment.

✔ Clear your calendar. Decide which meetings absolutely require your attendance. Your directs may appreciate your presence at a weekly meeting, but that may not be the best use of your time. Agree to attend the meeting only if they can prove your attendance is essential. Otherwise, have them send you updates or discuss meeting progress in your one-on-ones.

✔ Learn to say "Yes, and . . ." If a request comes from above, asking you to step up and take on a new responsibility that is not on your priority list, be sure to respond with, "Yes, and . . ."

This short phrase immediately demonstrates that you are open to opportunities, and it leaves room for you to explain and possibly negotiate your current situation. "Yes, that sounds interesting, and I'm currently leading the redesign of the financial systems. That's a high priority right now. Let's discuss what you need and determine if I'm the best person for this project." After learning more, you can decide whether you are the best choice or if you need to enlist the help of others. This might be a great chance to develop someone on your squad of direct reports.

✔ See if you can negotiate. Is the due date carved in stone? Can you put off what you are already doing? Do you need someone else to choose between these two priorities? Who can help you so you can help them?

Shift #11: From Clarity to Ambiguity

The further up the leadership ladder you go, the more ambiguity you are bound to experience. Getting accustomed to not knowing, to not having a clear path, and to unexpected continuous learning is a good thing. That said, your job as a leader is to create clarity for others in that ambiguity, to take all you've learned and create a path forward.

Let go of: Having all the answers.

"Leader as expert" is an outdated model. It's impossible to have all the answers given the complexity of our work environments. If this is your first promotion, you've likely been relying on others to set direction. Now it's your turn to step up and take point. If you get a little nervous, remind yourself it is entirely permissible not to know everything. If this is your fifth promotion, be to let go of the functional area you used to lead. Just because you had experience leading the marketing team doesn't mean you can talk intelligently about current marketing recommendations, especially if you are now head of strategy.

Instead, embrace: Enjoying the mystery.

✓ Seek the opportunity that comes from not having a clear path to follow. Imagine a future based on what is required rather than what has been done before. Innovation lives in welcoming the unknown.

✓ When you step into uncertainty, you create space for serendipity—unexpected encounters, discoveries, and connections. Humans always like to think they can predict the future. We can't. Allow yourself to be surprised by what comes up in the uncertainty.

✓ Embracing the strange and unfamiliar naturally pulls you from your comfort zone—always a little uncomfortable but frequently deeply rewarding.

✓ Begin to rely on others, including those newfound bonds you've created with your peers and leaders. Pick their brains to generate ideas. Learn how they've dealt with a lack of clarity.

✓ Recognize when you don't know. Admit it. Seek out a trusted brainstorm partner. Research and learn how others have navigated uncertainty.

✓ Remind yourself that even if you don't know now, you will eventually find your answers.

Shift #12: From Low Risk to High Risk

When you are a doer of work, you are allowed to make small decisions on your own. That's because your supervisor often mitigates the level of risk you encounter. If you are lucky, you will have a leader who will selflessly run interference for you and take the hit should something fail. As you take on greater responsibility, you will be relied upon to support others.

Let go of: Making decisions on your own.

The world today is highly volatile and complex. It is unlikely you will be making important decisions alone, even at the C-suite level. The sense of risk—the anxiety, questions, and ambiguity—does, however, increase the higher up you go. Your colleagues will be counting on you to support your ideas with data, facts, and details.

Instead, embrace: Proactively managing risk.

✓ Do your research. Test the data. Ask plenty of "what if" questions to anticipate possible stumbling blocks.

✓ Explore new ways of mitigating risk by tapping into your network, socializing ideas, and brainstorming with trusted advisors.

✓ Find someone in the company who successfully manages risk and ask them what they do to lessen it. Would they be willing to mentor you on this subject?

✓ Shift how you view risks, not as something to avoid, but as opportunities to make the company stronger. Remember, we don't know what we don't know. Your research may reveal new prospects and avenues for the company to pursue.

Shift #13: From Your Preferred Communication Style to Effective Communication

The best leaders communicate effectively. Some of my clients assume this means being "direct." However, being direct is often only effective when working with non-human systems or in times of crisis. It may feel great to be brutally honest with a peer or to get something off your chest, but your honesty is most likely just your opinion, not a statement of fact. If so, it will do more damage than good. And while you may feel righteous in delivering a tough message, if you've triggered defensiveness in another person, the message won't be heard. Brutally honest messages are notoriously ineffective. Effective communication means your messages are listened to, comprehended, and acted upon.

Let go of: Your preferred communication style.

Your style doesn't work for everyone. If you are a new leader or an experienced one, it's time to elevate your communication skills.

Instead, embrace: The power of language.

✔ When preparing to deliver a message, ensure that the context, priorities, and needs of your audience are clear to you. Tailor your choice of words and tone so your audience hears and understands what you are saying. Be brief and genuine in your messaging.

✔ Learn what is most important to the other person. David L. Bradford and Allan R. Cohen, authors of *Influence Without Authority*, refer to this as a person's "currency." Determine what they value most and use that to support your message.

✔ Learn to tell stories. Nothing pulls us in more than a good story. You can convey your point more effectively if you make it relatable.

✔ See yourself as a leader, someone who is both caring and factual. As you begin to own and internalize your role as a leader, your language will naturally shift.

Shift #14: From Doing to Leading

If it's not clear to you yet, your job has changed dramatically. You are no longer expected to do the work. You are expected to lead the people. Not only do your priorities have to shift, but your mindset does too. Begin to see yourself as a leader.

Let go of: Leading projects.

It's time to let your squad *do* and you *lead.* This means more than just leading projects, however. It means leading people who look to you for emotional support, clarity, direction, tone, and demonstration of appropriate behaviors.

Instead, embrace: Being a leader of people.

✔ Avoid the trap of thinking that achieving the work is more critical than serving the people you lead. (I fell into that trap, so you don't have to.) They are equal in importance.

✔ While others will view you through the lens of your new title, do your best to avoid doing that with your squad. Make a deliberate effort to see them as they are, not how you think they should be based solely on their titles. Do your best to see them as the complex adults they are.

✔ Learn what makes them feel proud at work. Ask them to describe a peak experience—a time when they were excited about what they were doing. Have them elaborate on the context of that experience. Ask them to remember the actions they took and how it felt. Listen carefully. As they share their peak experience, you'll learn what they enjoy doing, what gets them pumped, and how they want to feel about their work.

✔ Strive for constant improvement with your leadership skills. Assess your performance and challenge yourself to consistently improve.

Shift #15: From Pleasing to Positive Results

Naturally, following your promotion, you will want to please your supervisor, your squad, and peer group. Your responsibility now is to the company and doing right by it. That means your priority must be positive results, not just happy faces.

Let go of: Pleasing everyone.

Learn to challenge and question others in a collegial fashion. If you stay focused on solving the problem, your questions will reflect that.

Instead, embrace: Focusing on positive results.

✔ Yes, it is important to be liked. It's also important to be respected. You can have both. One way to create relationships with others is to be friendly, not necessarily friends.

✔ When working through an issue, remain focused on a common goal—something that will keep your conversation centered. What is it you and others are looking to achieve? How can you do that without getting into personal attacks? Keep the common goal in mind as you work through whatever issues arise.

✔ Apply the principle of noble intent—an assumption that everyone is doing their best and working toward mutual success. This sets the tone for your conversations and helps maintain a civil atmosphere.

✔ Practice being okay with your own self-satisfaction rather than counting on the opinions of others. Recognize that you'll get less immediate feedback (if you get any now) as you climb the company ladder.

I have not captured all the subtle changes that occur when a person is promoted, and your organization may have its own hidden expectations; however, this list is a good starting point.

After coaching for so many years, I can tell you that most of what you have learned so far can slow you down or even derail your progress. Marshall Goldsmith wrote the book *What Got You Here Won't Get You There* to drive home the point that every leader must let go of something and adopt something new to find new levels of achievement and fulfillment. If you have been recently promoted, now is your time to determine what to let go of and what to hold on to.

The Coach's Secret

Look out for these new, yet often overlooked, expectations as you continue your leadership journey. Transitioning from doing to leading involves numerous subtle shifts in mindset, behavior, and emotions. The sooner you identify what is different, the sooner you can accept it and decide how to move forward.

If you've been promoted, whether for the first or fifth time, pay attention to what this deeply experienced coach knows: Your title isn't the only thing that changes. Expectations of you are altered. You can't help but change too.

The next chapter introduces you to the ups and downs you may experience while you are transforming into the leader you know you can be.

3
YOUR TRANSITION

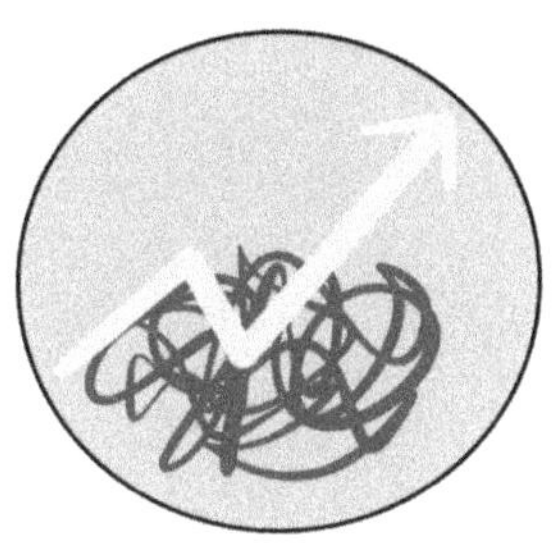

Let's get back to my client Chris. Recently promoted, he was having a hard time letting go of his old role. At the same time, he was struggling to figure out his new job. To help him, I introduced him to William Bridges's Transition Model.

Bridges (such an apt name for a model about transitions) distinguishes the concept of *change* from that of *transition*. He suggests we look at change as the trigger or starting point. In Chris's situation, the change occurred when he was told about his promotion. The point of change can be quick and instantaneous.

However, Bridges distinguishes a transition as being much slower and long-lasting because it encompasses what happens internally as you respond to the change. Therefore, Chris's resulting transition after his promotion consisted of the internal emotional journey he dealt with for months afterward.

It's worth exploring this model a bit more, especially if you've recently been assigned a new role.

These emotional transitions can also form the basis of your hidden metrics. It is helpful to anticipate both the large and small emotional steps you'll take as a leader during your transition. These signify forward movement and growth—great lessons from Life School!

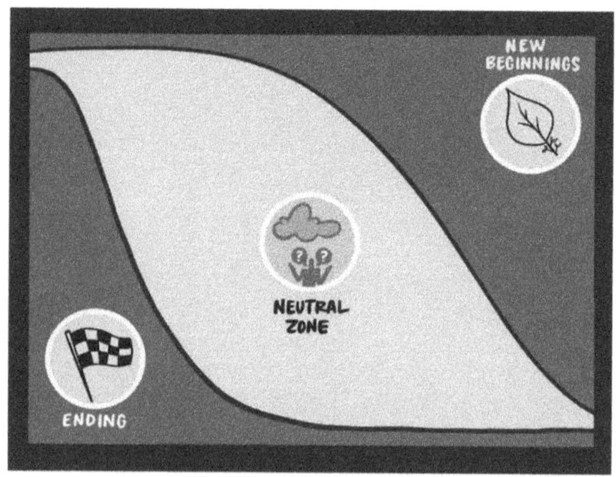

The Transition Model

Endings

The Transition Model begins with Endings. This is a period when we deliberately say goodbye to the reality that was. It's the time to bid farewell to being part of the squad, to being seen as the expert, and to doing the daily work. Chris, unfortunately, neglected to do this. He hung on as tightly as he could by showing up to meetings where he didn't need to be and interfering in decisions that should have been made by his directs.

Having a proper Ending means physically, emotionally, and mentally stepping away—and staying away—from the old so others can step in. Formalized ritual helps with this. There is something about a rite or ceremony that speaks to the human psyche. It's why we have elaborate and formal traditions surrounding events like births, weddings, and deaths. Creating a ceremony around the end of an era, a role, or a relationship can be healing. Such a ritual can remind us at a fundamental human level that something is over. It is time to move on.

Anyone can create ceremonies that formalize the end of a job. Elaine, the COO of a large pharmaceutical company, had been relocated to a new facility. As we worked together, I mentioned I admired her office décor. Behind her on the wall was a huge six-foot-wide photograph of the plant she used to run. Seeing this, I guessed, accurately, her heart was still at the old place.

I asked her where her mementos were of her new worksite. There were none. Realizing this, Elaine quickly understood she wasn't fully present, heart and mind, at the new facility. Her first step was to remove the large photo from the wall. She kept it rolled up but put away where she couldn't be reminded of her past.

To ritualize these periods of ending a role and letting go, my clients have purged their desks, file cabinets, and laptops; stored away all the trinkets collected from their previous gigs; and put away their old team T-shirts and hats. Some have removed their past awards or put them in a less prominent place to make room for future achievements. It's like putting away all the pictures of your old romantic partner. You may still have strong feelings for them, but deep inside, you know it's time to set them aside.

Use ritual to help you end what was.

The Neutral Zone

Now, you might think you are ready for the New Beginnings phase of Bridge's model. Not so fast. You have now just entered (cue music from *The Twilight Zone*) the Neutral Zone. I'm not a big fan of Bridges's name for this phase. There is very little that is "neutral" about it, as the Neutral Zone is characterized by significant ambiguity and unanswered questions. It is a highly messy, unsteady, and uncomfortable period.

Let's go back to Chris's story. Naturally, Chris had been given goals and metrics by his supervisor. Even so, he had a million questions: How does he ensure his squad does the right things? How should he spend his time with them now? What do they expect of him? What does his boss expect? How can he succeed now that he's not doing anything but sitting in meetings? What should his focus be? What is his purpose? How does he provide value? How does he stay engaged himself?

While the first phase, Endings, gave Chris something to do, the Neutral Zone demands you do nothing other than be patient. Yes, patient. (I can hear your silent screams from here.)

Most of us want to be doing something, to be in action, to feel forward momentum. But the Neutral Zone demands that you slow yourself down and wait for the answers to surface.

All the questions you have will eventually get answered. I promise. The Neutral Zone insists you learn the value of not knowing—something that may feel very foreign to you. If, like Chris, you have been the "go-to" or the one who has the answers, the Neutral Zone will be a challenge. However, this period of ambiguity presents an opportunity to learn more about yourself (Life School!) and your capabilities (the essence of self-discovery), and to remain open to whatever comes.

To help you survive this deeply uncomfortable phase, feel free to make a list of your biggest questions. Write them out. Check them off and celebrate when they get resolved. Watch as your list shrinks. (The Workbook has space for you to capture and track these questions.)

Go ahead and hold conversations that may move you closer to answers. Preface the discussion with, "I know it's early and we don't have all we need yet, but what do you think about . . ." This approach helps you collect some of the "negative space"—the information that fills in around the questions. Artists use this term to look at, not the image of what they are creating, but the context in which it is set.

The Neutral Zone can feel like it lasts forever, but I warn you, trying to move through it too quickly is risky. If you don't squeeze all the Life School lessons you can from the NZ, you may end up learning a harder lesson later.

For example, let's say you want to make a decision that you believe is necessary to make now. However, you haven't spent the required time getting to know what your peers, supervisor, and other stakeholders need from you—information that you can collect during the NZ—and are rushing the decision. Because you didn't involve key stakeholders or understand their needs, you may have to perform serious damage control. All because you wanted to get out of the NZ as fast as possible.

One client, Jackson, understood the value of being patient in the NZ. He created a mantra to remind himself, "I don't know now, but I will know eventually." Repeating this kept him in the present reality and reassured him that the Neutral Zone is temporary.

New Beginnings

The final phase of Bridges's Transition Model is New Beginnings. Once you feel you have most of your questions answered, you intuitively drift into this phase. This doesn't mean you haven't already been performing your new responsibilities. You probably have been. But in the New Beginnings phase, your new role and responsibilities start to feel comfortable, almost second nature to you. There are fewer unanswered questions and greater overall clarity. It feels like everything is falling together instead of falling apart.

How did Elaine ritualize her New Beginning at the new plant? She and I brainstormed ideas about how to celebrate her new role. Elaine came up with something fun: a vast collage of images from the new plant. With each new photo or business card, the new mural became a work of art. Creating it kept Elaine in the present, not the past. Elaine also found meaning in expressing herself through this new collage. It soon came to represent all the great relationships she was building.

Just like with the ending of something, ritual and ceremony can help you internalize the beginning. Now is the time to run a squad visioning workshop, to hold kick-off lunches or dinners. Splurge on new T-shirts, hats, and tchotchkes. Celebrate how far you've come!

But there is more to having a successful New Beginnings stage than just T-shirts and parties. There are two questions I ask my clients when they start a new position to help them transition into their beginnings phase.

The first question is "Do you feel you deserve it?" Lisa, a freshly minted CFO in the banking industry, felt like she didn't deserve her role. Because she was her predecessors' hand-picked lieutenant, she wasn't sure she was quite ready for the role when he abruptly quit. I know (and you know) that no bank that values its fiduciary responsibilities would ever promote someone to CFO who is not qualified. Lisa understood that intellectually, but she didn't feel as though she had earned that spot.

Lisa's lack of confidence showed in her interactions with her peers and with the shareholders. They were dismayed at her tendency to remain quiet when financial leadership was required. Through coaching, Lisa recognized that she had to respect herself before the board of directors would.

The first step was for her to take ownership of her leadership. She had to believe she was where she deserved to be. Once she started viewing herself as a senior leader who belonged in the C-suite, her interactions with others improved.

Do you feel you deserve this leadership role? If not, what do you need to do to convince yourself otherwise?

The second question is, "How do you define your leadership?" Most leaders have never thoroughly explored this question. Many have told me, "I lead by example." If that's your go-to response, let me tell you now that it is an entirely inadequate answer. (And some think I'm too soft! Ha!) At a minimum, leaders should lead by example. Even if you truly lead by example, are you clear on what example you are laying down?

Instead, I challenge you to be deliberate and thoughtful in creating the kind of leader you want to be. Consider positive role models you'd like to emulate, and don't forget the anti-role models who demonstrate behaviors you want to avoid. They offer a good contrast as you begin to refine your leadership. Decide what your reputation as a leader is going to be.

Sarah was a huge fan of Wonder Woman. Now, before you dismiss her role model as silly, remember Wonder Woman was meaningful for Sarah, not you. You may prefer a different superhero.

So, to continue: Sarah appreciated the virtues and values that Wonder Woman represented. Wonder Woman was empathetic, deliberate, and even skeptical at times—so skeptical she had a golden lasso that compelled people to tell the truth. She was brave and willing to do the hard things in the service of others. See how inspiring Wonder Woman can be?

In describing Wonder Woman, Sarah ultimately defined her own value system. Sarah wanted to be a leader who embodied all the qualities of Diana Prince, Wonder Woman's alter-ego, and more. That was our starting point to create a vision for Sarah's leadership style.

Now, you may have a real-life role model to follow. That's great. However, some leaders have not had the benefit of healthy and positive examples to follow and emulate. So, superheroes, film, TV, and novel characters work just as well.

Chris's Story

By the way, Chris did turn things around. He did it by deliberately setting hidden metrics for himself.

First and foremost, he began by saying farewell to his old role on the squad and embracing his new one. He decided how he wanted to grow as a leader, and he understood that his first step was to step back from doing the work. He was rigorous in limiting his daily involvement and began to trust his people to do what they needed to do. Chris also spent time defining his leadership philosophy. Once he was ready, he shared it with his directs. It was at that point that they knew what to expect from him.

I chuckle a bit now about how Chris's situation ended up. I met with his squad again about six weeks after my first meeting with them. They asked me to "change him back!" They had begun to realize that Chris's growth meant they would have to grow too. They hadn't appreciated how much they had relied on him. His squad now felt the real weight of the responsibility he had been carrying on their behalf.

A Word for the New Manager

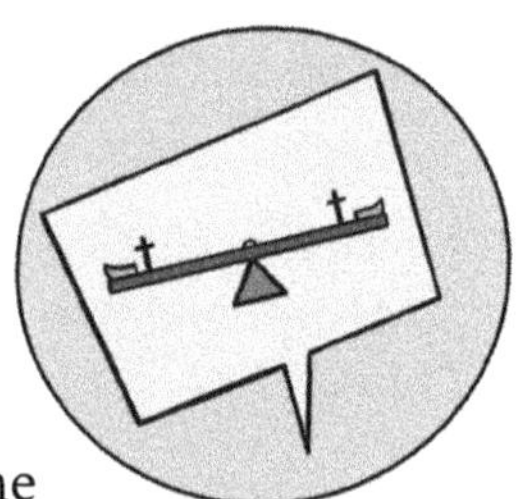

New managers, unfortunately, are often caught between expectations. This usually happens when a new manager leads a squad they used to be part of. Your supervisor may expect you to do and lead. This can be problematic. On the one hand, you must pay attention to day-to-day tasks, and you may still have activities that need to be completed. On the other hand, you will still be expected to become more strategic in your thinking and plan for the future.

It's not an easy thing to find the right balance. It does help if you know what to expect, however. Over time, you'll be able to reorganize those on your squad so they can take on more of your daily responsibilities, freeing you up to lead. Expect that your transition may take a bit longer, but don't worry, you will get through it.

The Coach's Secret

Coaches understand that change affects us all in so many ways. When a change occurs—like a promotion—it's not just about a new title or office or even a new set of responsibilities. Changes like these hit us hard, causing us to ask new questions of ourselves, such as, "What am I feeling? How are these emotions impacting others? What do I want to feel?" and "How can I see this change through and create success that matters most to me? How can I help others to succeed too?" And finally, "How am I growing?"

We've covered a lot so far: the value of metrics, hidden expectations, change, and transition. When you think about it, you may be going through a lot with your recent promotion. It gets easier now that you know what to expect. Take a breath and pause. Because we are now ready to look at the equation that will help you create your own powerful and life-altering hidden metrics.

4
THE HIDDEN METRICS EQUATION

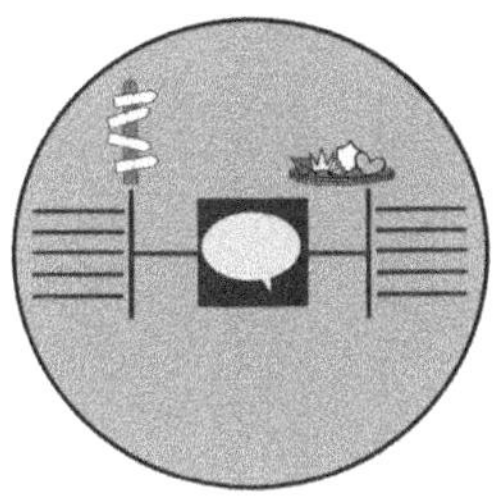

I knew from our very first call that Eric and I would hit it off. Eric wasn't just brilliant and ambitious; he had that rare combination of drive and genuine care for others that made him a natural leader. His squad's loyalty spoke volumes. And, as Eric told me about his role leading a group of ten thousand quality experts at a major pharmaceutical company, it was evident he wanted the best for them, his company, and the customer.

Eric was also a nice guy. Maybe a little too nice. He said yes a little too quickly to the requests that came his way, and he didn't push back nearly enough when challenged. Not surprisingly, Eric struggled to get buy-in on some of his ideas.

Eric held tightly to a vision that he very much wanted to see implemented. He believed his department deserved a seat at the senior leadership table, not for his glory but because Eric saw it as his mission to help enterprise leadership make better-informed decisions. The products his people quality tested weren't just items on a spreadsheet to Eric; they were treatments that could end up in someone's hands. His own elderly father's hands, for example. Truly, Eric's work was personal to him.

Seeking support for this vision, Eric naturally consulted his supervisor. While paying lip service to supporting Eric's growth, the supervisor's actions told a different story. He actively discouraged Eric from pursuing his vision. He interpreted Eric's goal as "too ambitious." Eventually, his supervisor told him flat out, "Stop talking about having a seat at the table."

Eric refused to be deterred. He knew this was the right vision for his function and the company. Eric had set himself an "audacious goal"—our reason for keeping it quiet and not discussing it with his supervisor. And it was my job, as his coach, to help him achieve that audacious goal.

Together, we dug deep into what truly inspired Eric. Soon, his vision crystallized: "My colleagues and I ensure the company makes the best decisions possible for our patients, customers, and stakeholders." This became the foundation for his hidden metrics—the meaningful measures of his success.

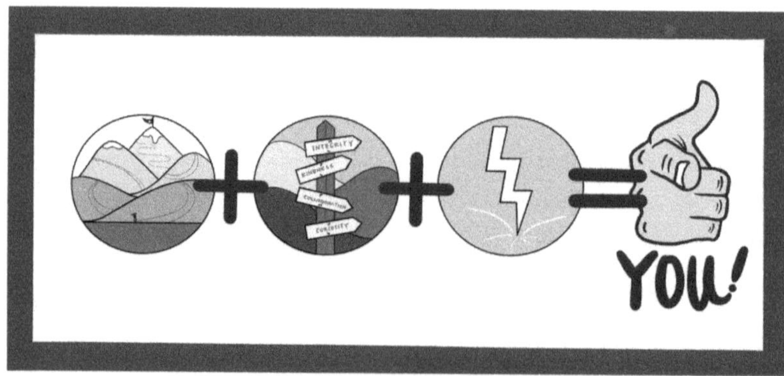

The Hidden Metrics Equation

Vision + Values + Strengths

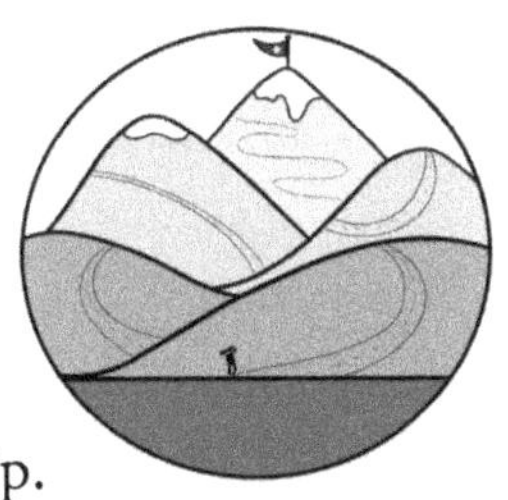

While businesses live and die by their bottom line, humans thrive on more personal metrics: vision, values, and strengths. These concepts form the foundation for the hidden metrics transformation for yourself and your leadership.

We begin with what it is you want to achieve, the vision for the future you want to create for yourself. Your vision may be like Eric's, bold and impactful. Or it may be a mindset shift, like Rajiv's, who didn't see himself on equal footing with the senior leadership team. Your vision defines how you want to be and what you want to do.

No one else has this vision. It is as unique as you are.

Many coaching clients have an idea of what they'd like to see happen in the future, but they don't often take the time to define, refine, and own it. Clarity of thought is needed to make that simple idea a reality. For our purposes, vision is where you are headed as a newly promoted leader. But vision alone isn't enough. You need two more essential elements: values and strengths.

Values serve as your guideposts. They are powerful statements of how you want to live your life. When you stray from them, you'll feel that internal tug pulling you back to center. But when you align with them, everything flows naturally. Think of them as your internal compass.

Then there are your strengths—the behaviors that not only come naturally but energize you. These create fuel for your journey, regardless of its duration.

Think about your best days at work. I bet they shared three common threads: you felt you were working toward something that was meaningful for you, you stayed true to your values, and you got to leverage your natural strengths. This equation—Vision + Values + Strengths—forms the foundation of your hidden metrics.

While the next three chapters provide detailed explanations of each element in the hidden metrics equation, the following offers a high-level overview.

Vision: Your Destination

Noah was a joy to work with. A director in a tech firm, Noah took everything we did in coaching and elevated it. He internalized the power of possibility. This came in handy since Noah ran a group of misfits—talented people who didn't always play well with others.

Still, Noah had a vision. He was determined to find a way to bring this diverse group of individuals together and create a truly high-functioning squad. Achieving this vision held meaning for Noah; if completed, it would bring people together and use their disparate skills to build amazing products. Remember AMeaningOfLife.org's Four Cornerstones of Meaning? Noah found significance in Love and Service.

Noah's vision didn't manifest overnight, but it eventually came to fruition. He deliberately spent time imagining what was possible. His squad's potential drove him forward and kept him focused. He had faith in them and in their ability to learn new ways of working, even though they weren't sure it was possible when he first shared his vision for a tighter, supportive squad. More than a few sets of eyeballs rolled when he brought it up repeatedly, but over time, his squad saw the value in the vision and eventually in each other.

For our visions to work, they must be both inspirational and meaningful. Visions are intuitively optimistic, describing a better future. Your imagined future needs to be so inspiring that it energizes you even during the toughest of times.

Values: Your Internal Compass

I admire all my coachees, but Malia is one of the most value-driven leaders I've ever met. The executive director of a charter school, Malia faced intense pressure after firing a popular but problematic instructor. Parents 

protested, threats were made, but Malia stood firm. She couldn't share the legal reasons behind the dismissal, but she knew she'd made the right call.

Why? Because Malia's values were crystal clear: putting the children first, keeping the school viable, and ensuring fairness across her diverse stakeholder group. These values kept her heading in the right direction through each storm she faced. As tempted as she was to walk away from all the drama (pun intended—it was a theatre teacher after all), she knew she couldn't live with herself if she did.

We learn our first values from our parents and family. They teach us either directly or indirectly what is most important in life. Over time, you may realize these same values no longer work for you. Perhaps your family was highly competitive, but you now feel as though collaboration is more important to you. Your values evolve from your life experiences. Being deliberate about what is most important to you is a crucial part of growing up and becoming a self-actualized adult.

When you operate counter to your values, your body feels it. It's like wearing your shoes on the wrong feet—everything feels off. That's why defining your values is crucial, especially when stepping into leadership roles. Your values become the foundation of your leadership philosophy. When you deviate from your values, you and the people you lead will feel the dissonance.

As you create your hidden metrics, your values will serve to keep you aligned and on track to achieve your vision.

Strengths: Your Natural Fuel

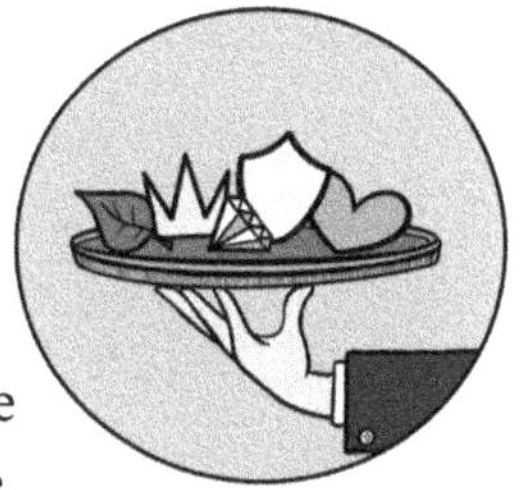

For at least a hundred years, management and performance consultants have concentrated on fixing weaknesses. However, new research indicates that this approach serves to perpetuate weakness, rather than repair it. Why? Because there's no energy there. Let me explain through another client's story.

Senior sales professional Hugh and I met during a leadership workshop I was facilitating. As part of the program, his 360-degree feedback report indicated what he did well and identified one area he could improve. The report suggested he needed to challenge the status quo more frequently. Hugh and I made great progress on the goals he was excited about. But, despite a year of working with me and trying various approaches, Hugh had made little progress in this area. Why? Because the idea of pushing back on others didn't energize him. He got no positive buzz from the idea of questioning how things were done.

When we began to work together, I asked Hugh whether challenging the status quo was something he enjoyed. Not surprisingly, his answer was, "No." However, he insisted that he should work on this since it was his lowest score. At the end of the engagement, I wasn't surprised when he admitted to being disappointed at his lack of progress. Hugh felt defeated, ignoring the substantial progress he had made on other goals. I reminded him again that his focus should be on what he does well, not what he does poorly. It is fully permissible for all of us to choose which goals we set and work toward. Eventually, Hugh set aside that energy-zapping goal. Together, we celebrated what he did achieve through coaching, specifically those goals that originated from his strengths.

The reality is that we thrive when we operate from our strengths—those behaviors that we perform well but also energize us. Think about activities in which you excel. Notice how one win creates a positive feedback loop; doing well feels good, which motivates you to do more, leading to even better performance. This becomes a cycle you want to repeat.

When we apply our strengths, we feel inspired, stimulated, dynamic, and charged up. As you build your hidden metrics, we will want to make certain these energizing behaviors are present to keep you flowing with momentum.

Alignment of All Three Elements

Your hidden metrics emerge from the intersection of these three forces: your meaningful vision (destination), values (guideposts), and strengths (fuel). When aligned, they create a compelling vision for both work and life.

ERIC'S HIDDEN METRICS

VALUES — SAFETY, COMMUNICATION, AUTHENTICITY, COLLABORATION

MAKING the BEST DECISIONS for EVERYONE

STRENGTHS — CURIOSITY, STORYTELLING, RAPPORT BUILDER, COUNTERPOINT

Eric's story illustrates this perfectly. Remember, his vision centered on ensuring the best decisions for the company's patients. Eric found meaning in Love (building relationships), Discovery and Exploration (stretching himself), and Service (doing right by others). Because his vision held personal meaning for him, Eric was determined to keep his goal in mind, despite what others, including his boss, might think.

But there was more. Eric used values such as safety, communication, authenticity, and collaboration to foster stronger relationships with his peers and senior leadership.

Because Eric was such a nice guy, which made it easier for his ideas to be dismissed, he relied on authenticity to guide him as he re-established relationships with everyone at work, including his boss. You see, when Eric was being accommodating, he was not being fully authentic. He wasn't staying true to himself—the very definition of authenticity. In the past, when he was agreeing to decisions he didn't believe in, his mind and heart were screaming, "This is wrong! We can do better!" He vowed to do better himself.

To stay energized, Eric also relied on his strengths, such as curiosity, storytelling, rapport building, and the ability to present a counterpoint. When he applied these strengths, he found a natural energy. It made him want to use these strengths repeatedly.

With a clear vision (better overall decision-making), values (safety, communication, authenticity, and collaboration) and applying strengths that revitalized him (curiosity, storytelling, rapport building, and counterpoint), Eric was able to create a set of metrics that mattered—not just to his company's bottom line, but to the lives of patients like his father.

Eric's hidden metrics—too audacious to share—gave him a plan to follow. He began setting up regular meetings with supporters and other meetings with those who disliked his ideas. He put his energy toward nurturing relationships, determined to remain fully authentic. As hard as it was, Eric learned to push back and offer counterpoints to arguments. He shared data and stories to get people to see what he saw.

Eric did obtain that coveted seat at the table, and remember that sitting at the big table was never the goal. For Eric, it was about influencing enterprise-wide decision-making for the good of the company and patients. His vision for himself and his squads became a reality because he was now seated in the room where the decisions were being made.

A Couple of Caveats

There are a few critical points to consider as you develop your hidden metrics.

As much as I'd like to 100% guarantee your success with these, ultimately the metrics you set and the effort you put in determine your progress, just as they do in coaching. You can work with the most incredibly skilled coach, but if you don't do the work, nothing will change. How far you go is always in your hands.

Also, although I've presented the creation of hidden metrics in a linear, step-by-step fashion, they often don't manifest in that manner. Don't be surprised if you find yourself revisiting your vision to refine what you truly want, selecting different values, or relying on other strengths. All that is okay. Life is not linear, no matter how much we try to make it seem that way.

The Coach's Secret

Professional coaches understand that hidden metrics—the ones you often remain quiet about—are fruitful because of what is already deep within you: your vision, values, and strengths. The magic is in envisioning a meaningful future, discerning what is most important to you, and implementing what you already do well to propel you forward. The beauty of hidden metrics is that they measure what truly matters to you, not just what shows up on a spreadsheet. Hidden metrics are the accurate indicators of success that matters—they are the ones that tell you you're not just doing well but doing right.

In the following three chapters, you will find powerful questions and activities to help you uncover and define your vision, values, and strengths.

5
MANIFESTING YOUR VISION

What Do You Want?

One of the most powerful questions in the world is "What do you want?" It sounds simple, but most people struggle to answer the question. They respond with a list of things they *don't* want. For example, I hear people say, "I don't want to fail," "I don't want to be poor," or "I don't want to lose this opportunity." Declaring what you don't want is not the same as stating what you do want. The negative phrasing doesn't work when it comes to crafting a vision because you are putting your energy and attention on what you don't want.

Every hidden metric you create is grounded in this important distinction: What you want is more powerful than what you don't.

Susan David, a prominent Harvard professor and author, refers to the things we don't want as "dead people's goals." No one wants to live a life of avoidance; we want lives of creation and meaning. We want to leave this life knowing that we have left a mark in some way.

So, I ask you, "What do you want?"

When we spend time carefully considering and naming what it is we want, the desire moves into the realm of the possible and probable.

Your desire becomes the vision for the hidden metrics equation. Whether you refer to it as your end goal, objective, outcome, or destination, it is based on the answer to the question, "What do you want?"

Ultimately, the vision you are creating has deep, personal significance for you. Others may be affected by the outcome, but the vision I'm challenging you to imagine is grounded in your special wisdom.

The thing is, we don't live in a vacuum. Others around us have their ideas and expectations for us. It's tempting to simply go along with what others think, rather than trusting our own intuition and wisdom.

Oughts versus Ideal

Richard E. Boyatzis, renowned professor at Case Western University, writes in his book, *The Science of Change*, about the difference between the Ought Self and the Ideal Self. As he describes it, "The Ought Self is a version of a future imposed or coming from external sources to the person." In the context of our careers, others, including senior management, have ideas about what you should be creating for yourself and what you ought to do.

> *...OUR HOPES, DREAMS, AND DEEP SENSE OF PURPOSE ARE THE DRIVERS OF SUSTAINED CHANGE AND LEARNING.*
> —RICHARD E. BOYATZIS

Rather than assuming those folks know what is best for you, learn to trust your own judgment. Get to know your ideal self. According to Dr. Boyatzis, your ideal self is the emotional driver of intentional change. It is grounded in an image of a desired future, hope, and strengths. Sound familiar? I hope so.

Your ideal self speaks to you all the time. Will you listen? Your wise inner voice already knows what it is you need to create. If you listen carefully, your vision will gradually present itself.

If, however, you listen to everyone else, your vision may be buried under the *don't wants, oughts,* and *shoulds* of daily expectations.

Internal and External Shoulds

While Boyatzis uses the word *ought*, most of my clients tend to use the word *should*. Have you ever noticed how often you say the word *should* every day? How many times is it used by others? "I should go to the gym." "I should clean the house today." "I should try to get to bed earlier tonight." "I should finish up that report before I leave work."

Whenever I hear *should* from a client, I understand two things: 1) It's not what this person wants to do, and 2) Someone else has set this expectation for them. The Ought Self is winning out.

The word *should* signals that a deeper coaching conversation is required. Remember Hugh from the prior chapter? He was never going to "challenge the status quo." We were only working on that goal because a standardized report gave him a low score on that leadership quality. In his mind, he should challenge the status quo. The report told him he ought to do it. It was not what he wanted to do.

In addition to the external shoulds or oughts that you hear from others who don't understand you or your dreams, some internal shoulds or oughts may surface as you craft the vision for what you want to create.

When clients use the word *should* about themselves, it can signal that they don't accept their current reality. Instead, they wish for a different existence, an existence they believe should exist but doesn't. This can lead to resentment, an emotion that rises from the refusal to accept what is.

"She's a vice president! She should know better than to make that decision." Or "I expect more from him. He's a certified tech." These are examples of complaints that are set in a reality that does not exist. In these quick examples, neither the vice president nor the tech knew better. That is the reality. Just because you assumed they should know better doesn't make it accurate. It's on you to accept what is. If you refuse to accept how things really are, then you will likely begin to resent these people, who are probably just doing the best they can.

Also, the use of the word *should* can be a red flag that our egos have taken control. The ego speaks with a lot of shoulds, as in "I should be promoted." Or "I should get more recognition for what I do."

When I hear these red flag statements from my clients, I get curious. Coaching questions start pinging around inside my head. "Do you truly want that promotion or just acknowledgement? What is it about being a leader that attracts you? What kind of leader do you want to be? How will your life be different if you got it? What does it do for you? How might it work against you? What's the downside?" As your coach, I will ask as many questions as needed to determine whether your ego is running the show or if this is your ideal self doing the talking.

I've mentioned the "ego" several times already. It's worth defining it so you can keep it under control.

Your Ego

Your ego is your sense of "me"—the part of your mind that feels like the real you. It's what makes you feel like a distinct person with your thoughts, feelings, and experiences.

Your ego acts like the CEO of your mind. It makes everyday decisions, figures out how to handle problems, and manages your interactions with the world around you. When you decide what to wear, how to respond to a text, or whether to take a new job, that's your ego at work.

Mostly, your ego keeps you feeling like the same person over time. Even though you're constantly changing and growing, your ego maintains that inner sense of "this is me." Your ego isn't good or bad; it's a regular part of being human that can work better or worse depending on how it developed and how well it's balanced with other aspects of who you are.

A healthy ego enables you to navigate life confidently while remaining flexible and open to learning. You can make decisions, set boundaries with people, and handle both wins and losses reasonably well. Problems arise when your ego becomes either too big (thinking you're always right, needing constant praise, believing you deserve that promotion) or too weak (trouble making decisions, letting others walk all over you, feeling worthless).

When your ego is using the word *should*, it's a sign that it might be taking over. It might be whispering things that aren't true, opinions that are grounded in what you fear or don't want most.

Fear and the ego are deeply intertwined because the ego's primary job is to maintain your sense of being a separate, coherent you. Your ego is a survival mechanism. It's constantly scanning for anything that might threaten your identity, safety, or sense of control. This creates a baseline level of anxiety about maintaining your place in the world and protecting who you think you are. A threatened ego may trigger a fear of rejection, failure, embarrassment, or any experience that might shatter your self-image.

Your ego has different defensive mechanisms. When threatened, your ego typically responds with defensiveness, blame, rationalization, or aggression. It might also flee through avoidance, denial, or numbing behaviors. These responses often create more problems than they solve.

The ego can also become hypervigilant, constantly anticipating threats and creating elaborate strategies to avoid potential dangers.

This can lead to chronic anxiety, perfectionism, or controlling behaviors.

What would you say is your ego's typical response to being threatened?

Who Is Talking?

Discerning the voice of your ego versus your ideal self is an important skill. Understanding the differences between the two is absolutely necessary to developing your self-awareness. It takes practice to recognize the different qualities of these inner voices. What follows are some guidelines to help you distinguish between your ego and your ideal self.

The Ego's Voice:

✔ Feels urgent, reactive, and often fear-based. It frequently uses language like, "I have to," "I should," or "What if . . ."

✔ Comes from a place of comparison and competition. It might say things like, "I'm better than them" or "I'm not good enough"—constantly measuring against others or past versions of yourself.

✔ Concentrates on external validation and immediate gratification. The ego asks, "What will people think?" or pushes for quick fixes and shortcuts.

✔ Creates internal drama and conflict. The ego voice often feels scattered, anxious, or demanding. It tends to catastrophize situations or make everything about maintaining your image.

✔ Sounds like internalized voices from your past—critical parents, demanding teachers, or societal expectations you've absorbed. It often carries the emotional charge of old wounds or conditioning.

Your Ideal Self's Voice:

✔ Feels calm, clear, and centered, even when addressing difficult situations. It doesn't rush or panic but offers steady guidance. There's often a quality of spaciousness around it.

✔ Speaks from your core values and long-term wellbeing rather than immediate fears or desires. It might say, "This feels right" or "This aligns with who I want to be."

✔ Focuses on growth, connection, and contribution rather than just self-protection. It considers the bigger picture and how your choices affect others and your future self.

✔ Offers creative solutions and possibilities rather than warnings or demands. There is a sense of curiosity and openness.

✔ Has a quality of loving firmness. It can be direct about what needs to change without being harsh or mean.

Tips to Help:

✔ Pay attention to the physical sensations that accompany each voice. The ego often creates tension, shallow breathing, or agitation in the body, whereas your authentic voice typically comes with a sense of expansion, deeper breathing, or a feeling of settling.

✔ What emotions are surfacing: excitement or anxiety? The latter comes from the ego.

✔ The voice of the ego will often get louder and more insistent when ignored, while your more profound wisdom tends to remain patient and available when you're ready to listen.

✔ Notice the timeline each voice focuses on. The ego is often stuck in past resentments or future worries, while your deeper wisdom tends to be present-centered with a healthy consideration of long-term consequences.

✓ Check the motivation behind the voice. Is it trying to avoid something painful, or is it moving toward something meaningful?

✓ Take a moment for quiet reflection or meditation. Your authentic voice often becomes clearer when you step away from the noise and reactivity of daily life.

Speaking of taking time to reflect, the following section presents suggestions to help you create space for deep reflection.

Uncovering Your Vision

For the purposes of hidden metrics, consider what you want to create for yourself and others at work. Imagining your future doesn't require any special tools or steps. It just takes a little bit of time dedicated to you. In addition, feel free to use this same approach to help you clarify what you want in your personal life, too, because as much as we try to maintain a separation between work and life, the two are inextricably entwined.

So, how do you get in touch with that wise voice of your ideal self?

Get quiet.

Go outside. Take a walk. Sit in a park, on your deck, or on your back porch. Go someplace where you can be alone. No distractions. No phones. And if possible, refrain from using headphones or playing music. The challenge is to be with yourself. Listen as your inner voice whispers your truth about what is best for you and others.

Bring a notebook. Take in the fresh air with three deep breaths. Hold each until you feel your heart beat. Release the air slowly.

When you feel relaxed and centered, ask yourself, "What do I want?"

I admit that is a big question and perhaps too big to answer right away. Here are some more specific questions that might spark meaningful answers:

1. What would an ideal day be like for me?

2. Who do I want to surround myself with? What are these people like?

3. What satisfies me most at work? When am I happiest?

4. If I could wave a magic wand, what would I want to change? What would stay the same?

5. What have I always known I've wanted but never achieved?

6. What needs to change for me to leave a positive legacy?

7. What is the bold move that I am afraid to make but want to make anyway?

8. If I weren't afraid, what would I do?

9. What would make me proud of myself?

10. What do I really want for myself and others?

If you find yourself falling into the trap of thinking about what you don't want, flip it on its head. If you don't want to be stressed, then its opposite is "I want to be at peace." If you find yourself focusing on not failing at work, then shift your perspective to "I want to succeed in my current role."

Visions, at their core, are aspirational. Good ones paint a clear picture of what's possible. Great ones pull others in. Here are a few tips to consider as you write down your vision:

✔ Visions are more powerful when they are written in the present tense. Our brains want to register this as something that already exists. Use "I am a leader who . . ." not "I will be a leader who . . ."

✔ Clarity is key. Be as specific as you can. Include dates, times, numbers, etc. I have a good friend who is a talented facilitator of presentation skills training. She has declared the number of workshops she will deliver this year and the exact amount she will earn from each. Her vision feels more real to her because she's allowed herself to imagine the details.

✔ Resist getting hung up on whether something is probable and instead decide it is possible. Our egos will try to protect us from taking unnecessary risks but that shortchanges us. We can create amazing things if we believe in the possible.

✔ Read your vision aloud—daily. Internalize it so it becomes part of you.

Remember, when we act from a deep understanding of what it is we want to create or solve, so much more is possible for us. To make the possible viable, your hidden metrics are always centered on your desires, interests, and needs.

Manifesting Your Vision

There's more to setting a vision than writing it down. To make it real, you must manifest it.

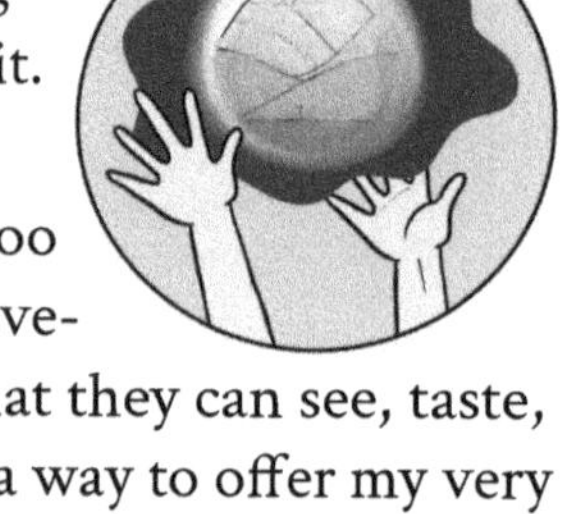

Throughout my career as a coach, I've walked a fine line between being too woo-woo and too practical. I fear that I'll turn off my five-sensory leaders, those who only believe what they can see, taste, touch, hear, and smell. Inevitably, I still find a way to offer my very left-brained, logically minded clients concepts that could be seen as spiritual. Over the years, I've introduced hesitant clients, including CEOs, to meditation, immutable laws, and energetic modalities—always to great success. One of my guiding principles as a coach is to use what works for my client, regardless of the woo-woo factor.

That's why I'm introducing you to the topic of manifestation. It works. Let me share some examples.

Jim Carrey, actor and comedian, wrote a check to himself for $10 million for "acting services rendered" in 1985 when he was broke. He dated it for Thanksgiving 1995. He kept the check in his wallet and achieved that level of personal and professional success by his target date.

Richard Branson, founder of Virgin companies, grew up with nothing. He carries a notebook with him and jots down business ideas and goals. He credits this practice with helping him build his companies across multiple industries.

Sarah Blakely, founder of Spanx—which sold for $1.2 billion in 2021—wrote down her goal to invent a product and become an entrepreneur. She famously wrote her business plan and goals on yellow legal pads while working as a door-to-door salesperson.

All these famous and successful people started their careers as unknowns with only their visions to drive them forward. Like them, you can manifest your vision too.

What does manifestation mean exactly? Think of it as breathing life into your declared desires, goals, or outcomes through focused belief and action.

Imagining what's possible and writing your vision down is the first step in manifesting your future. However, more is needed to bring it to life. After all, the process of identifying your vision and writing it down is an intellectual, mind-based activity. To fully manifest it, your entire self, body, emotions, and language need to be involved.

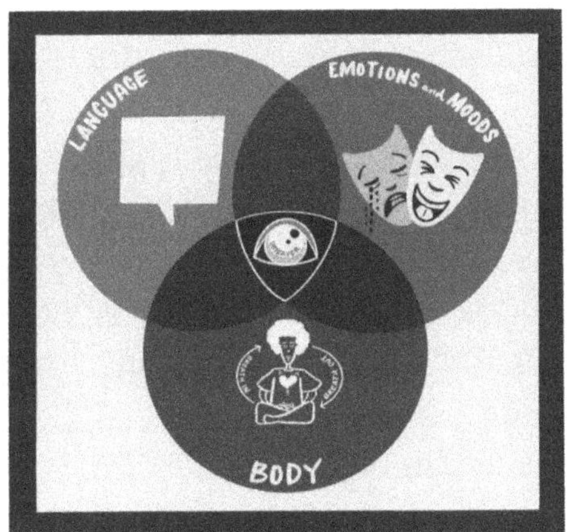

The BEL Model

The Body, Emotion, Language Model

As a coach, I rely on the Body, Emotion, Language (BEL) Model to not only help you alter your behavior but also to create new, healthy habits—to make your vision a reality and ground and support your declaration by inviting in all you are.

✔ **Body:** Your physical self, body language, how you dress, your energy levels, or lack thereof, your health and fitness.

✔ **Emotions:** Your feelings and moods.

✔ **Language:** Dreams, ideas, belief systems, inner chatter, as well as the way you use language when you speak—aka everything that's going on in your head.

The BEL model is based on what is observable—our physical selves, our emotions, and our language—which represents what's going on in our heads. When we align all three elements, we become fully ready to create something new: mind, body, and heart.

In applying the BEL model, you've already engaged your mind by imagining what's possible for you and your role. So, let's involve your body next. When you are ready, stand up with your shoulders back. Speak your vision aloud in a clear and confident voice. Repeat this until your delivery feels authentic and easy.

As you declare your vision aloud, notice the feelings that may surface. How do you describe the emotional energy that arises within you as you declare your chosen future? Is it excitement? Optimism? Relief?

Next, allow yourself to imagine what it will physically and emotionally feel like when your vision comes alive. How great will that be? Can you feel yourself smiling because what you want finally happened? Do you take pride in yourself for making it a reality? Can you feel the satisfaction that comes from creating this new future?

Hold on to these sensations for as long as you can.

Practice this daily. Bring your vision into reality by practicing the integration of your body, emotions, and language.

Go Deeper: More Visioning Questions

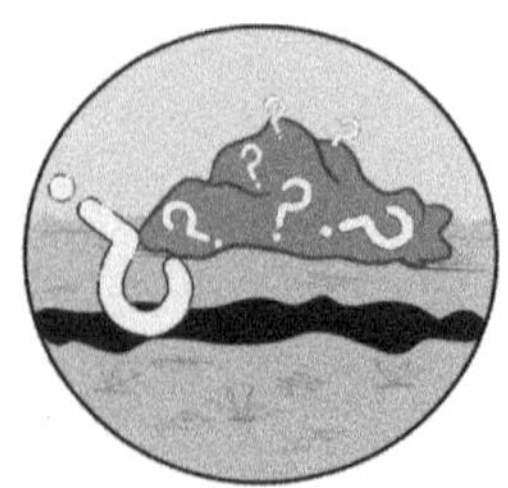

I'm a coach. I ask questions for a living. Here are some additional questions you can ask yourself to deepen your vision.

The following inquiries are more specific to work environments and are designed to create more clarity for you. They have been grouped by the motives ("Why Hide"s) covered in Chapter 1, but I encourage you to read them all. You never know which one may spark a brainwave that takes you somewhere unexpected but exciting. Take your time with these. Allow your vision to come alive gradually and fully.

Motive #1: Fear of Asking for Help

Why it matters: You may feel concern that requests for help may be misinterpreted or that you will be seen as incompetent. What do you want so much that you'll risk asking for the help you need?

- ✓ Since external pressures, including meetings, are unlikely to change, what can you do to reclaim your authority?

- ✓ How do you want to feel at the end of your workday? What must you create for yourself to feel energized and engaged?

- ✓ What do you need to delegate or let go of to achieve more in your new role?

- ✓ What is an ideal day for you? What actions do you take throughout the day that have meaning for you?

- ✓ Think about new ways to work with your peers in other departments. What emerging cross-functional collaborations could become critical to your success? How can you position yourself as a valuable partner in these relationships?

- ✓ How can you encourage others or create a culture that values asking for help?

Motive #2: Obsolete Mindsets and Behaviors

Why it matters: You may worry that these will cause you embarrassment and limit future progress.

- ✓ When you think about the most inspiring leaders you've encountered, what specific qualities and actions stood out to you and how did they influence their squad's achievements?

Reflect on concrete examples and the lasting impact these leaders had. To have fun exploring this question, don't forget your superheroes. What superheroes or novel characters do you most admire and why? How have you become like them over the years?

✓ What habits, behaviors, or mindsets are blocking you from wildly succeeding? Look for clues in the feedback you've received. How would it feel to release these limiting beliefs and attitudes?

✓ What is recurring feedback you've gotten for years? What would it look like if you finally moved beyond it, either by deciding once and for all that it's not relevant or finding a way to use your strengths to resolve it?

✓ What is the daring or bold move you hesitate to take that will change how you lead or interact with others?

✓ If your performance were to become recognized as the gold standard in your field, what would have led to that recognition? What are the concrete outcomes that would demonstrate your exceptional value and impact?

Motive #3: Long-Term Goals

Why it matters: Do you have goals that are so long-lasting, you want to create something meaningful for yourself in the short term to stay inspired and energized?

✓ What is essential about the work you do? What is most meaningful to you about the long-term project or goal you've been assigned? How can you make sure you experience that meaning on a regular, if not daily, basis?

✓ How can you find growth and fulfillment along the way? What relationships can you build? What trust needs to be repaired? What new learning can you acquire as you work toward this goal?

✓ One, two, and three years from now, what would meaningful success look like for you and what tangible changes would others notice in how you operate?

✓ When you achieve this long-term goal, what lasting impact do you want to have made on individual squad members' growth and development along the way?

✓ What cultural elements or values do you want to instill that will continue benefiting the squad and organization long after the project is complete? Think about sustainable practices and mindsets.

✓ What stories do you want former squad members to tell about their experience working with you when they're in senior leadership positions themselves? Think about the formative experiences and lessons you can create.

✓ What traditions or regular practices could you establish that would energize you as you attend to your long-term projects and goals?

Motive #4: Confidential Feelings

Why it matters: You may fear revealing to others how discouraged and disengaged you are.

✓ What is it you are afraid to share with your supervisor about yourself, fearing it could change their perception of you or work against you?

✓ When did these attitudes first arise? What seemed to trigger them? How are they working for you or against you?

✓ If you feel one way now, what feeling would you like to experience instead? How will the new emotion or attitude benefit you?

✓ When did you last feel inspired and engaged? What was happening then? How were you contributing? What were you learning?

Motive #5: Audacious Goals

Why it matters: Some goals are so big that others can't fathom them happening.

✓ What is the big idea you want to implement? It may be so big it frightens you a little. Or it may be so unexpected that the organization doesn't quite understand its potential.

✓ Who benefits from this idea? What will they gain? What will you gain if it is implemented?

✓ How can you align your idea with the problems or challenges your organization faces? How are you uniquely positioned to solve them?

✓ What unique strengths and experiences do you bring, and how can you leverage these to make a meaningful impact?

✓ How will you feel later in life not having gone after this audacious goal?

Motive #6: Feedback Isn't Relevant or Accurate

Why it matters: You disagree with the feedback you've received but still want to grow and improve.

✓ What feedback have you gotten that feels right to you?

✓ What feedback has triggered you somehow? What specifically in the feedback bothers you? What is your guess as to why it does? Is there something there to explore? Is your ego actively protecting you now?

✓ If this is feedback you've received before, how will you finally choose to either correct it or let it go?

✓ What is the one thing everyone seems to miss about you and your capabilities that you want to spotlight going forward?

✓ How can you appreciate yourself and your gifts and not worry about making this other person happy?

Pulling It All Together

There's a lot to bring together to create an actionable vision and turn it into reality. By listening to your ideal self, asking powerful questions, writing meaningful declarations, and internalizing your vision through body, emotions, and language, you will launch your future and establish the foundation for your hidden metrics.

Here are some examples of powerful, effective, and successful vision statements:

- ✔ "I am a leader of leaders who challenges, coaches, and develops them to higher levels of performance and satisfaction."

- ✔ "I am a fearless leader who models how to handle challenging situations with a steady and calm demeanor so we can all focus on what we need to do."

- ✔ "I assume positive intent as I work with my colleagues, so we can build a healthy workplace where we listen carefully to one another."

- ✔ "I adopt new mindsets and corresponding behaviors that serve my squad so we can all succeed."

- ✔ "I celebrate the small wins so I can remain inspired as I achieve the long-term goals."

Your Rallying Cry

Your vision doesn't need to be fancy or long. A rallying cry serves as a powerful internal and external communication tool, making visions accessible and actionable. Keep it short, punchy, and inspirational. Think Nike's "Just Do It" or Apple's "Think Different."

Set aside time to draft your full visioning statement and then create a shorthand way of making it memorable and meaningful for you. Here are some examples:

The Full Vision	**Rallying Cry**
Be the leader all the best players want to work with.	Attract the best!
Make the best decisions for our customers.	Right decisions!
Be fearless in discussing and mitigating risk in our work product.	We love risk!
Confront each other with positive intent in mind each time we are in conflict.	It's the issue; it's not personal.

The Coaching Secret

Coaches recognize the magic of silence. We are trained to remain quiet after we ask questions, while you ponder and consider your answers. You can do the same. Allow yourself the time to be alone for a bit and listen for the whispers that tell you what is best for you. Give yourself the silence you need to imagine a fantastic future where you feel inspired, alive, and engaged. This is what you are working towards. A future that you define, you create. A future that has resonant meaning for you. Then, allow yourself time to imagine what life will be like when you achieve that goal. Experience the feelings of fulfillment, satisfaction, and pride.

Now, let's examine what will keep you on your path toward that vision—your values.

6
LIVING YOUR VALUES

The Power of Your Core Values

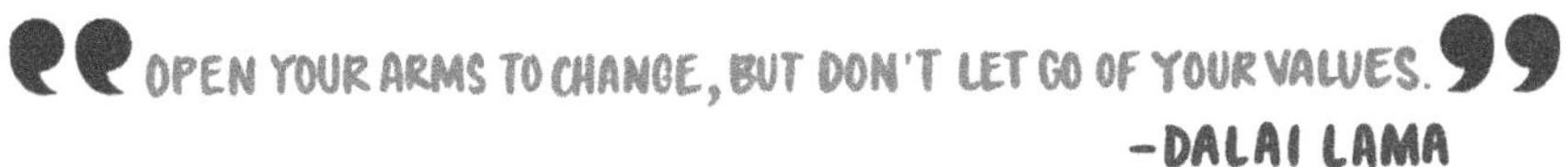

On his twenty-third bombing mission over North Vietnam, Lt. Commander John McCain was shot down, breaking both arms and a leg. Taken prisoner of war, he was tortured and then sent to the infamous Hanoi Hilton, or Hòa Lò Prison. His captors refused to treat his injuries. He suffered through two years of solitary confinement. Despite having been severely beaten, almost daily, over the five years of his imprisonment,

McCain refused to accept early release, perceiving that as a propaganda coup for the North Vietnamese. Instead, he insisted his fellow POWs be released in order of their capture date.

Later, McCain ran for US House and Senate. He earned the nickname "Maverick" because of his tendency to deviate from more conservative colleagues. Instead, he voted and acted in alignment with his own value system.

No matter your political leanings, it is easy to see Senator John McCain understood the supremacy of his personal and professional values. They are what kept him alive through it all.

Values: Your Personal Guidance System

Values aren't just abstract concepts; they're the fundamental beliefs and principles that guide every decision you make. They determine what you consider right and wrong. They influence who you trust, where you work, how you lead, and what gives your life meaning.

Think of your values as the personal guidance system—not GPS, but PGS—running in the background of your life. Most of us inherit our initial values programming from our parents or early influential figures. As we mature and gain life experience, we begin to update this system by letting go of outdated beliefs and embracing new ones that better serve our authentic selves.

Unfortunately, few of us ever consciously examine our programming. We live on autopilot, wondering why certain situations, jobs, or relationships feel so uncomfortable, never realizing it's because we are not sticking to our core values.

> **A HIGHLY-DEVELOPED VALUES SYSTEM IS LIKE A COMPASS. IT SERVES AS A GUIDE TO POINT YOU IN THE RIGHT DIRECTION WHEN YOU ARE LOST.**
>
> — IDOWU KOYENIKAN

Identifying Your Values

There are several different ways to define the concept of values. Brené Brown, academic, researcher, and author of many books, describes values as the principles that guide our behavior and decisions, essentially serving as our personal North Stars. In her book *Dare to Lead*, Brown writes that values clarification is essential for wholehearted living and courageous leadership, noting that ". . . daring leaders who live into their values are never silent about hard things." She could have easily been talking about John McCain.

Values are the beliefs that are most important to us, and they dictate how we want to live and treat others. They serve as our PGS, our signposts, that keep us moving toward our vision and goals.

The world's many philosophers have thought long and hard about human values. Values can fall into different categories. Some represent principles to which we are held accountable, such as honesty and integrity. Still other embody actions we can take, as in being kind and generous. And others address ways in which we want to aspire to live, such as in abundance and connection.

As a leadership coach, I created my own list of values based on common leadership competencies. In using the list, let the headings speak to you. Seek out what is necessary to supporting you as you manifest your vision. For example, if your vision is to "be a leader of leaders" you may want to look at the Mentor/Develop Others, Relationships and Delegation groups first.

Then, select the values under that heading that resonate with you. Feel free to explore the other values that are listed under other competencies too. If it helps, say the words aloud. Notice how you feel emotionally and physically when you speak them. Highlight or circle those that hold meaning for you.

I suggest identifying ten values. Then, narrow your list to five.

Hidden Metrics Values List

DECISION-MAKING

Accountability | Competence | Confidence | Critical Thinking | Data Analysis | Decisive Action | Goal Setting | Initiative | Judgment | Problem Solving | Responsibility | Strategic Thinking | Wisdom

MENTOR/DEVELOP OTHERS

Accountability | Caring | Competence | Generosity | Growth | Learning | Patience | Service | Teaching | Wisdom

EMOTIONAL INTELLIGENCE

Compassion | Confidence | Emotional Regulation | Empathy | Grace | Humility | Patience | Present Focus | Respect | Self-Awareness | Self-Discipline | Self-Expression | Social Skills | Understanding | Vulnerability

INFLUENCE

Caring | Charisma | Clarity | Competence | Confidence | Critical Thinking | Humor | Inspiration | Persuasion | Presence | Recognition | Social Skills | Understanding | Vulnerability

RELATIONSHIPS

Belonging | Caring | Collaboration | Community | Compassion | Connection | Curiosity | Diversity | Empathy | Friendliness | Inclusion | Love | Loyalty | Respect

MEANING

Altruism | Ambition | Connection | Continuous Learning | Faith | Hope | Legacy | Loyalty | Love | Making a Difference | Purpose | Respect | Spirituality | Vision

ADAPTABILITY

Agility | Continuous Learning | Creativity | Curiosity | Flexibility | Growth Mindset | Innovation | Resilience

ETHICS

Corporate Responsibility | Dignity | Ethics | Fairness | Honest | Integrity | Justice | Respect | Responsibility | Social Responsibility | Stewardship | Transparency | Trustworthiness

FEEDBACK

Active Listening | Ambition | Caring | Continuous Learning | Curiosity | Factualness | Growth Mindset | Honesty | Receptiveness

DELEGATION

Accountability | Communication | Confidence | Empowerment | Growth Mindset | Responsibility | Trustworthiness

COMMUNICATION

Active Listening | Assertiveness | Authenticity | Clarity | Compassion | Conciseness | Honesty | Truth | Understanding

BUSINESS ACUMEN

Achievement | Competence | Competition | Customer Focus | Efficiency | Excellence | Financial Security | Innovation | Resourcefulness | Strategic Thinking | Success | Wealth

SOCIAL RESPONSIBILITY

Citizenship | Community Service | Environment | Generosity

SECURITY

Consistency | Protection | Reliability | Risk | Safety | Security | Stability

PERSONAL EXCELLENCE

Ambition | Commitment | Determination | Discipline | Perseverance | Work-Life Balance

EXECUTIVE PRESENCE

Accountability | Charisma | Confidence | Excellence | Honesty | Respect | Trustworthiness

STRATEGIC CAPABILITIES

Ambition | Big Picture Focus | Collaboration | Continuous | Learning | Critical Thinking | Data Analysis | Future Orientation | Growth Mindset | Innovation | Long-Term Vision Risk

Congratulations! You have a first draft of a values list. Be sure to keep these close. Add these to your desktop or put them on sticky notes in plain sight so you can readily refer to them.

Remember, these will keep you on your path toward your end goal, your vision.

What If I'm Not Like John McCain?

Thankfully, most of us will never be tested in the same way McCain was, so let me share Stephanie's story. A vice president in charge of safety for an energy company and the only woman on the leadership team. Since we are both women, it wasn't surprising to either of us that she had started getting push-back from her peers and senior leaders. She was hearing the same complaints we always hear about women Stephanie is too soft, too emotional and, somehow at the same time, too direct and forceful.

Stephanie's performance was stellar, but the "guys" weren't all that comfortable with her. On one level this makes sense. Safety is often at odds with Operations in large organizations. She was sure their discomfort with her was because she held them accountable—and she was a woman in a man's world.

Stephanie had gotten this feedback shortly after a senior leadership team meeting. Ironically, during this very same meeting, her male counterparts openly cursed and yelled at each other. She had to ask, who was really too emotional?

To deal with this inconsistency or hypocrisy—no matter what you want to call it—Stephanie needed to rely on her own personal values to stay steady. Intuitively, she knew what felt right for her, but she had never been deliberate about exploring and naming what that was.

Stephanie created a vision for herself that went beyond what was expected by her boss, the CEO. It read, "I am responsible for the safety of every person we employ, and I do not allow others' mindsets and behaviors to interfere with that."

Using the Hidden Metrics Values List, Stephanie came up with the following:

✔ **Safety:** Physical safety for the employees, fiduciary safety for leadership.

✔ **Relationship Building:** Creating new business relationships grounded in respect, investing in existing relationships.

✔ **Future Orientation:** Focus on what is best for the employees and the company.

✔ **Humor:** Finding the humor in every situation.

✔ **Patience:** Remain patient, knowing it may take the other executives awhile to come around.

✔ **Competence:** Continue to be competent; elevate skills as needed.

✔ **Confidence:** Hold on to self-confidence no matter the pushback.

✔ **Emotional Regulation:** Hold it together when peers are losing it.

✔ **Curiosity:** Be curious about your peers; keep asking questions.

Stephanie's top five values included relationship building, future orientation, safety, humor, and patience. She decided she would approach each of her peers on a one-to-one basis rather than in a large group. She'd spend time asking questions, getting them to laugh, open up, and relax around her. That way, she hoped, once they were back in the board room, they'd listen to her ideas. She'd also socialize her ideas ahead of time, especially with those peers who may be problematic. In their one-on-one conversation, Stephanie decided to avoid discussing the past and instead focus on what the company needed going forward. No one likes being made to feel wrong, least of all her peers. So, Stephanie agreed that staying positive about what they could create as a team would help.

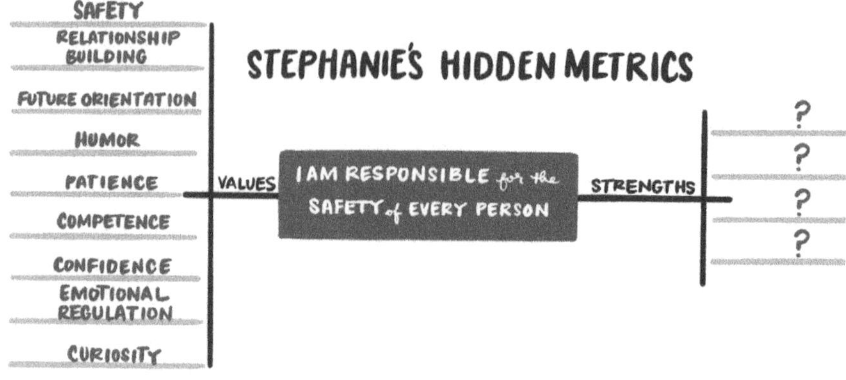

As she worked toward her vision, Stephanie relied on this list. In fact, she made a deliberate effort to stick to her values until her peers stopped complaining and began to view her as a valuable partner. If there was a day she wasn't feeling patient, for example, Stephanie made a concerted effort because her vision was so meaningful to her. She reminded herself that people's lives were at stake.

Along the way, Stephanie cut herself some slack. She recognized she couldn't change their behavior; they'd have to want to do that out of respect for her. She wanted them to view her as a colleague, not a safety scold.

When clients like Stephanie take the time to identify their core values, their decisions become easier, and boundaries become stronger. They feel good about themselves and how they show up at work and in life. That was how Stephanie felt. She began to see that adhering to her own value system was critical to her own self-regard.

Feeling Your Values

When we deviate from our values, we know it. At the very least, we recognize that this is not how we want to be. At a maximum, we may feel a sense of self-betrayal or guilt.

John McCain, as strong as he was during his internment in the Hanoi Hilton, did eventually break. After his release, he commented that we, as humans, all have a breaking point. He openly regretted signing a forced confession. He made sure never to do it again despite multiple demands from his captors. He strongly felt he had betrayed his fellow prisoners of war and himself. There are times when I still mentally kick myself for not having followed my own set of values. We are human, we are frail, and we all have that "breaking point." Identifying and sticking with our values creates not only our reputation but also our character.

The Coach's Secret

Coaches know that in every interaction—whether easy or taxing—your values are at work. They're the magnetic force that pulls your internal compass back to true north. Values form your Personal Guidance System to keep you from getting lost or sidetracked. That's why they're essential tools in creating your hidden metrics—those deeply personal standards of success that transcend external validation.

In the next chapter, we'll explore how the energy derived from your unique strengths keeps you in flow as you pursue these hidden metrics.

7
APPLYING YOUR STRENGTHS

Aadhya was an effective leader. She relied on an established set of "go-to" strengths to achieve her assigned goals. Trusted and reliable with a strong work ethic, Aadhya took her work seriously—a bit too seriously. All her energy was devoted to achieving her assigned goals. Unfortunately, like so many others, she believed that good work alone would be enough to get her promoted. (She's not alone. This is common misconception. It's never enough to just do quality work.)

Aadhya knew what she wanted and had a hidden vision for herself: to be promoted to a level where she could influence the direction in her department. Through our work together, she clarified her values: work ethic, quality, and working collaboratively, among others.

But as strong and smart as she was, Aadhya wasn't fully tapped into all her strengths. She was so focused on the obvious ones required by her function that she neglected to use the ones that would naturally elevate her reputation and her position.

Defining Strength

Most of us have been taught to think about strengths all wrong. We're conditioned to view them as merely what we're good at—the skills, talents, and abilities that yield competent performance. But this definition is only half of it.

Cappfinity, a pioneering positive psychology research organization based in the UK, notes that a strength contains three essential components with a simple equation:

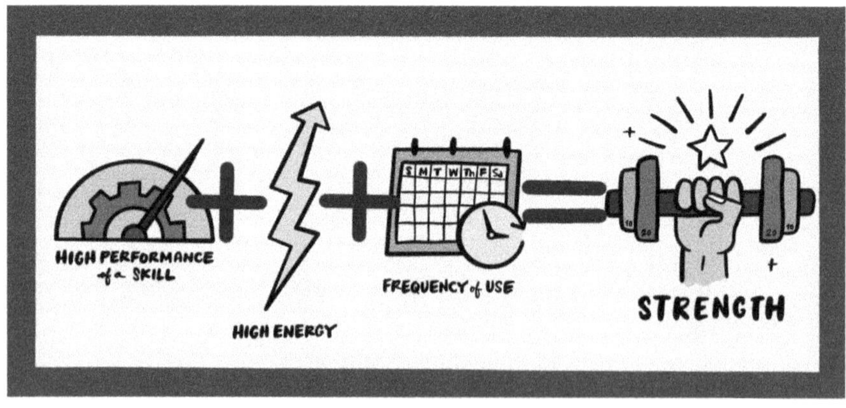

The Definition of Strengths

This equation explains why some people excel at their jobs yet feel perpetually drained while others seem to have boundless enthusiasm for their work.

The concept of strengths comes from a relatively new field of study: positive psychology. Rather than studying mental illness and psychopathologies, positive psychology explores what makes human life meaningful. This includes areas of research such as strengths, positive emotions, relationships, and self-actualization.

Since we spend most of our waking hours working, it makes sense to examine how we use our strengths in the workplace. A considerable amount of research has been conducted in this area. The results are evident and compelling. According to Gallup, producer of CliftonStrength Assessment (formerly StrengthsFinder), people who operate daily from their strengths:

✓ Experience six times more engagement at work.

✓ Are 15 percent less likely to quit their jobs.

✓ See 12.5 percent greater productivity.

✓ Maintain these benefits over time, while those fixated on weaknesses show declining performance.

How Strengths Can Work for You

I know from personal experience how helpful it is to understand one's strengths.

Fifteen years ago, I experienced a period of burnout. I had been operating my coaching practice the same way for a long time. I told myself that if I had to listen to one more leader tell me how bad they had it, I'd scream. I was bored out of my mind. What to do? Well, hire a coach, of course!

The first thing my coach did was offer me the Strengths Profile (now called Skills Discovery) from Cappfinity.

The results showed that I was overusing certain behaviors that weren't strengths—they were weaknesses. A weakness is defined as something you perform poorly that de-energizes you. Upon reviewing the results, it became clear to me that I was investing my energy in aspects of my job that I wasn't particularly skilled at and didn't enjoy.

Oh, you want to know what my weaknesses are? I don't mind sharing.

✔ **Competition:** I dislike competing with others. It drains my energy, and I never feel like I win, regardless of the game.

✔ **Work Ethic:** I hate working long hours. I value my free time.

✔ **Adherence:** I'm *not* a rule follower. I can follow the rules, but I'll still complain about it forever.

The approach a traditional boss or management consultant might take would be to get me to focus on "fixing" these weaknesses. It's not that I didn't know how to do these things; I just don't enjoy doing them. I get no energetic buzz from performing them.

Think about it: When any of us do something poorly, we feel inadequate. That pessimistic feeling makes us resist doing it again, creating a downward spiral. Instead, Strengths Theory encourages you to act from a position of strength. When we apply our strengths, we get a natural burst of energy that we want to experience again and again.

My coach turned my attention away from my weaknesses and toward the list of activities and behaviors that energized me. After some discussion, it was apparent I was also overusing strengths that I was good at but that had become repetitive and boring to me.

Surprisingly, I was relying too heavily on Compassion. Yes, coaches need to be compassionate, but even I need a break from that occasionally. Another strength that I was using too frequently was Action. I derive a lot of energy from being active, from jumping right in and getting the work done. But being too active can also sap my energy.

Between my reliance on my weaknesses and over-reliance on some strengths, the reason for my burnout became clear.

Next, we examined the strengths I was good at that brought me energy but which I wasn't utilizing for some reason. One of these, Adventure, stuck out for me. It was like finding a key to a door that I had forgotten about. In my personal life, I love to explore and do new things. I realized I wasn't permitting any Adventure in my coaching practice.

My coach got to the point: "How can you bring more Adventure into your work?" I started to come up with new ideas, not just for the client, but for me, so that I could experience Adventure again in coaching. I felt a burst of excitement and a willingness to try new techniques as I coached my clients. I came up with everything from new quotes on my email signature to coaching outside to trying new coaching methodologies. Within no time, I was reinvigorated.

Harnessing infrequently used strengths immediately energized me. We all have more within us than we realize. Recognizing that we can do more, be more, and give of ourselves in new and exciting ways empowers us.

Weaknesses Have Value Too

Generally, we coaches advise against spending too much time, energy, and attention on trying to fix your weakness. It's counterproductive. However, identifying and understanding them is also important.

One of my favorite activities to conduct with teams can feel counterintuitive and a little risky for some people as it requires everyone to be a little vulnerable.

I require every person to share their weaknesses with colleagues and supervisors publicly.

The anxious energy in the room is usually palpable. People shift uncomfortably and giggle with nervousness. But what happens next can be transformational.

Let me share a real story that resulted in a positive change. I facilitated a strengths workshop for a team of IT professionals. It was Alan's turn in the hot seat. He cleared his throat and admitted, "I absolutely hate following rules and procedures. My weakness is in Adherence." (I immediately liked him!)

His teammates erupted in knowing laughter. "That explains everything!" one colleague exclaimed.

For months, his peers had wasted countless hours trying to coax Alan into completing standardized reports on time. Now they understood—this wasn't a case of laziness or disrespect. This task, grounded in rules and procedure, fundamentally drained him.

Alan added that he had other great strengths, including Innovation, Curiosity, and Counterpoint. When he was at his best, he was asking questions, challenging processes and creating new systems.

His supervisor and team quickly realized they were trying to force a round peg into a square hole. Together, they reset expectations for Alan and found a way to automate some, though not all, of the forms.

Think about it. If his team hadn't learned about his weakness, everyone's frustration would have increased, and his colleagues would have become resentful. No one bothered nagging Alan anymore. The forms got completed, and importantly, Alan felt seen and recognized for his unique gifts.

As you create your hidden metrics, make certain you are drawing on your revitalizing strengths not the ones that sap your verve. If you operate from your strengths daily, your momentum will naturally increase. This will give you the oomph you need to reach your hidden goal, to achieve that invisible set of metrics.

Identifying Your Strengths

Historically, we've concentrated so much of our mental energy on fixing what we've been told is wrong that sometimes it's hard to know what we do right. You can begin to discern some of your strengths simply by answering these questions, which are based on the work done by Alex Linley, PhD, of Cappfinity.

1. Performance Clues

✓ What activities do you master faster than others around you?

✓ When do you find solutions that others miss?

✓ What tasks do people seek your help with, even outside your formal role?

2. Energy Signals

✓ During which activities do you lose track of time?

✓ What work do you look forward to, even when exhausted?

✓ What topics animate you when explaining them to others?

3. Usage Patterns

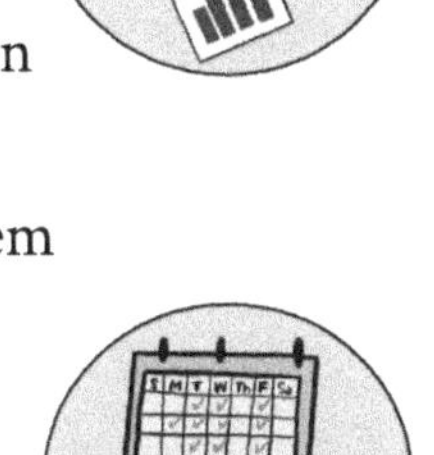

✓ What activities do you make time for, even with a packed schedule?

✓ Where do you volunteer or step up without being asked?

✓ What abilities do you seek opportunities to use?

4. Success Patterns

✓ What common approaches appear across your proudest achievements?

✓ What positive feedback do you consistently receive?

✓ In what situations do you feel most confident and capable?

CappFinity also has a great list of strengths to choose from. See page 187-191 of the Workbook.

If you'd like to use a more formal approach to identifying your toolbox of strengths, here are some assessments that are easily accessible. They are all grounded in the same principles found in Strengths Theory and positive psychology. These are the three instruments I work with most frequently.

✓ **Skills Discovery:** Formerly the Strengths Profile, this places eighty strengths into four categories to help you understand how to use them. Your go-to strengths, which you rely on daily, are Realized Strengths. Learned Skills are strengths you perform well but are now draining for you. Weaknesses, as I've mentioned, are actions you do poorly that de-energize you. The fourth category is Unrealized Strengths, those actions that you are great at and energized by but for some reason, you aren't using them frequently.

✓ **VIA Inventory of Strengths:** This basic instrument is free, but you can also purchase additional, more detailed reports. The VIA measures and ranks twenty-four character strengths that you can apply at home or work. Each character strength falls into one of six broader virtue categories.

✓ **CliftonStrengths:** Most popular in the United States, this system ranks thirty-four strengths and places them in four domains: Executing, Influencing, Relationship Building, and Strategic Thinking. There are three different CliftonStrengths assessments available depending on your needs.

Aadhya, Continued

If you remember, Aadhya took her work too seriously, yet she still yearned for that promotion. In her office conversations, she was all about status reporting and what needed to be accomplished. There was no small talk, no chit-chat, no curiosity about the people sitting in front of her. Her focus was entirely on the work.

Aadhya believed her hard work would get her noticed, but it was the exact opposite of what was required. If she wanted to be promoted, she would have to demonstrate a higher level of capability, specifically in interpersonal skills.

During an early coaching session, I asked her about her friends at work. Aadhya admitted that she didn't have friends from the office; her friends were mainly family who lived nearby.

I knew Aadhya had children, so I asked her how her young daughter made friends. Aadhya laughed and said, "She just walks up to people and starts talking with them. She's so good at that. She's fearless." I challenged Aadhya to see what she could learn from her daughter about making friends.

Two weeks later, Aadhya had mined two new strengths: Building Rapport and Curiosity.

Up to that point, she hadn't permitted herself to be curious or to make personal connections because, like so many of us, she was only looking at half the picture—the metrics set by her bosses and upper management. Aadhya thought that if she hit her targets, that would be enough to get her promoted. But it's not. All leaders must demonstrate strengths beyond the technical ones required by their jobs. At a minimum, they must demonstrate that they can get along with others. So, Aadhya committed to this: She was going to start making friends and connections at work.

This clarity prepared her to begin the hidden metrics process. Aadhya created her vision statement: "I am an approachable, respected, and supportive technology leader who assists in guiding the division as we make important decisions." That's a mouthful, so she shortened it to "Friendly and Competent Gets Best Decisions."

And we identified the values she holds most dear:

✓ **Belonging:** Giving herself permission to belong to other groups besides her family.

✓ **Continuous Learning:** Always challenging herself to learn more about herself, people, and things.

✓ **Competence:** Continue to develop her capabilities.

✓ **Curiosity:** Be curious about the people and the work they do.

To these, we added three strengths:

✓ **Rapport Builder:** Establishing rapport and relationships with others quickly and easily.

✓ **Listener:** Listening intently and focusing on what people say.

✓ **Connector:** Making connections between people by instinctively making links and introductions.

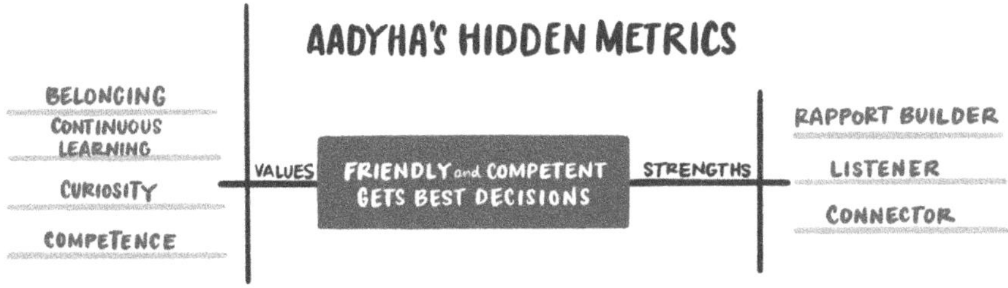

Aadhya began by keeping her values close by; she attached a sticky note to her monitor. If, at the end of a day, she didn't feel she had stuck to her values, like being curious enough with a colleague, or she didn't feel as though she had learned anything new, she would try again. She also began each meeting asking herself, "How can I be a rapport builder, listener, and connector today?"

After about a month, I checked in with her boss. He commented on how much happier she seemed at work; she was laughing and smiling more than she ever had. He did, however, have one concern. It seems that two European leaders appreciated Aadhya's work product and enjoyed her personality so much that they wanted to transfer her to their offices. Rather than lose her to them, her boss now recognized that he'd have to do something more significant to keep her around. Aadhya was promoted later that year. Her hidden metric became a reality.

Aadhya created her future vision by declaring it, utilizing a strong value system, and getting energy from previously unused strengths.

Now, of course, Aadhya's promotion was really a bonus. What she wanted most was to be a voice in the room when decisions were made. So, once her promotion came through, we created a new batch of hidden metrics for her to make sure her new leadership role reflected what was most meaningful to her.

The Coach's Secret

Coaches don't waste time on what you are doing wrong. We know a fool's errand when we see one. Instead, we help you discover ways to apply what you are good at—your strengths.

As you build your metrics—those significant personal goals that fuel personally meaningful success—your strengths become your greatest allies. Unlike willpower, which depletes with use, strengths generate energy the more you engage them.

Because the truth is this: your most tremendous potential lies not in fixing what drains you but in harnessing what energizes you. Your strengths aren't just what you do well; they're the unique combination of talents that make you come alive.

When you align your vision and values with your strengths, you don't just perform better, you create a sustainable source of motivation that carries you through challenges. You experience what psychologists call "flow," that state of energized focus where work feels less like effort and more like expression.

I invite you to read how a few of my coachees pulled it all together in the following case studies.

8
CASE STUDIES

If you have spent time contemplating a vision, clarifying what you value, and identifying your strengths, you are ready to create the hidden metrics that will keep you involved, engaged, and inspired.

Let's walk through three examples that demonstrate the hidden metrics equation in practical use.

Jackie

Context: Jackie was a Senior VP of Sales at a recruiting firm, having been promoted the year before. She'd been with her employer for a long time, so very little surprised her anymore. Each year, she was expected to meet or beat the sales goals set for her, and each year she did just that. The reason we started working together was that she felt disconnected and uninspired. Jackie knew that her blasé attitude would eventually interfere with her success. She needed to find a way to get out of her funk and turn it around. Jackie had an idea that she thought would get her energy back on track. But first, she had to let go of satisfying just her boss's requests and embrace those things that were meaningful to her.

Relationship with supervisor: Jackie reported to the CEO. They'd worked together for over twenty years. They understood each other and worked well together. They would say they were friendly, but not necessarily friends.

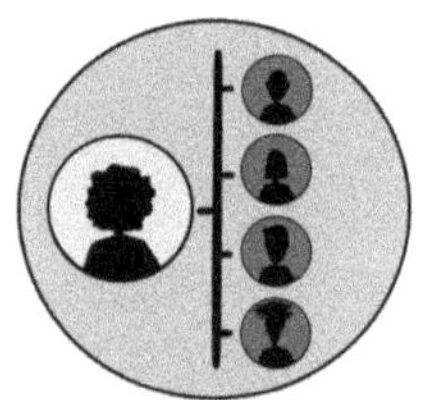

Assigned goals: Just as in previous years, Jackie had sales targets to meet. She used to get fired up seeing what the following year's challenge might be, but lately, these weren't inspiring to her. Jackie was ready to do something more meaningful.

The motive for keeping it quiet: Having already spoken to the CEO about her interests in doing more than selling, Jackie knew he wasn't a fan of the idea. He had learned to count on her high numbers and wasn't interested in seeing Jackie spend her time in other ways. But Jackie had a vision she felt compelled to follow. She didn't want to let it go.

Jackie's vision: Jackie wanted her work to mean more than just exceeding her sales targets. The emotional buzz she used to get from being the top salesperson didn't hold as much meaning anymore.

She was much more excited about developing the skills and deepening the knowledge of her less-experienced colleagues. That's not to say that Jackie didn't want to win and bring in the work. She certainly appreciated the bonus checks that came with being number one. As we spoke, Jackie shared a vision that included both growing others and earning a good income for herself and her family.

Jackie thought through her vision and composed it this way: "I find personal satisfaction and meaning in selling the work and helping others succeed too."

You'll notice Jackie's vision statement is written in the present tense, as if it were already happening. This approach convinces the psyche that the vision already exists, making it feel even more achievable. She created a stronger emotional connection to her future.

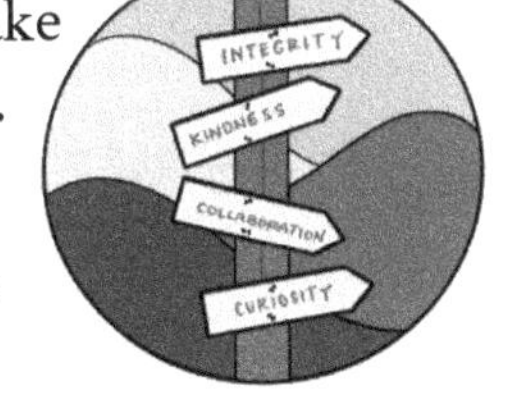

Rallying cry: "We all succeed!"

Jackie's values:

- ✔ **Financial stability:** She still wanted to make her sales goals, so that value never changed.

- ✔ **Stewardship:** Jackie wanted to help those around her, not just focus on her success as a sales professional.

- ✔ **Service:** Jackie was already active in her neighborhood and church; now she saw an opportunity to be of service to her colleagues.

- ✔ **Success:** Jackie wanted to continue to be successful financially.

- ✔ **Flexibility:** Jackie valued the flexibility her role provided her. It was the only way she'd be able to make this vision a reality.

Jackie's values may seem to be in opposition to each other. How could she fulfill her values of financial stability and success and still achieve these others: stewardship, service, and connection? We had to examine her definition of each of these values more closely. After some deep and serious thought, Jackie realized she had been sacrificing other vital values to satisfy just one. She chose to live from all her values.

Service now had greater meaning for Jackie. She watched the younger salespeople doing their best but still not meeting the goal. Jackie felt an internal tug between wanting it all for herself and knowing that she could change someone's life by helping them achieve more. For Jackie, it felt wrong to ignore their needs. Her Personal Guidance System was activated!

Eventually, Jackie was willing to bet that an increase in sales for the younger salespeople would offset any gains she might have made herself.

Jackie's strengths:

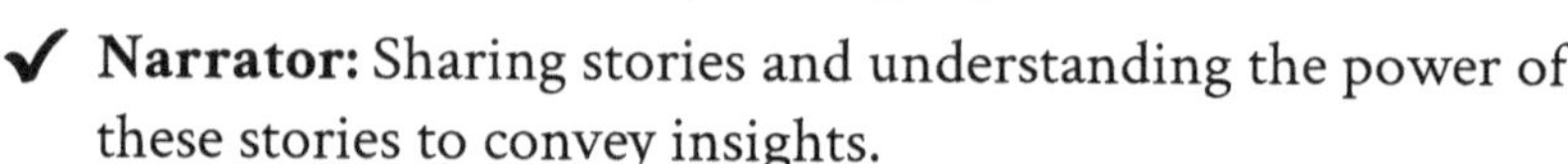

- ✓ **Rapport Building:** Establishing rapport and relationships with others quickly and easily.
- ✓ **Relationship Deepening:** Forming deep, long-lasting relationships with people.
- ✓ **Narrator:** Sharing stories and understanding the power of these stories to convey insights.
- ✓ **Planning:** Making plans for everything.
- ✓ **Listening:** Listening intensely and focusing on what people say.
- ✓ **Persistence:** Never stopping, even when things are tough.
- ✓ **Optimism:** Always maintaining a positive attitude.
- ✓ **Connector:** Seeing and creating connections between people, making links and introductions.
- ✓ **Time Optimizer:** Maximizing time and getting the most out of the time available.
- ✓ **Work Ethic:** Working hard; putting a lot of effort in all you do.

Remember that Jackie got rewarded with an energetic buzz every time she used her strengths. This is what would galvanize her as she worked toward her vision.

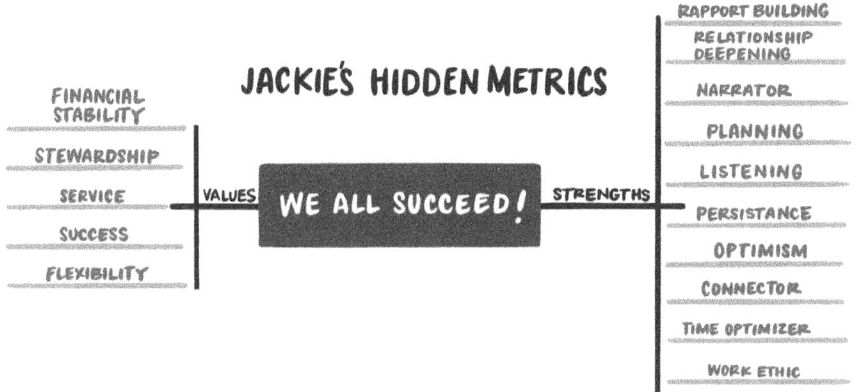

Jackie's hidden metrics: Here is the final set of hidden metrics for Jackie, along with which of her strengths she would be employing for each metric.

1. Set up meetings with younger salespeople. (Stewardship, Service + Rapport Building, Optimism, and Time Optimizer.)

2. Plan a schedule to work with no more than two salespeople at a time for no more than four hours a week. (Flexibility, Stewardship, Success + Time Optimizer, Relationship Deepener.)

3. Track protégée improvements and sales increases. (Financial Stability, Stewardship, Success + Planning, Persistence, Time Optimizer.)

4. Continue for three months and re-evaluate at that time. (Financial Stability, Stewardship, Success + Planning, Persistence, Relationship Deepener, Work Ethic.)

5. Keep track of personal sales activity; don't let anything slide. (Financial Stability + Optimism, Time Optimizer, Planning.)

Jackie's outcome: Three months later, Jackie was happier and more satisfied. Not only did she help improve the capabilities of two people, but their sales increased. This was great news for them, the company, and Jackie.

What's equally as important is what happened to Jackie over that ninety-day trial period. In every meeting—even boring ones—she found herself listening differently. Instead of just taking the information in for herself, she thought about how to discuss the content with her protégées later. Jackie started asking questions that she imagined her mentees might have. Her overall level of attention and involvement escalated. Plus, Jackie was also on the lookout for opportunities that might be ideal for her students. At no point did her numbers drop. She pushed herself to find new ways to be efficient. And since she was never spending more than 10 percent of her time (four hours a week) mentoring, she saw this as a win-win.

After that first quarter, she graduated the first two protegees. After six months, she graduated two more. She took a month off from mentoring to spend more time on her accounts but was back at work with two newbies after thirty days.

Jackie reported that she was excited about going to work. She was making connections, teaching others, cheering them on, and celebrating when they hit their goals. She found meetings to be more fun and engaging. Jackie had found the meaning she was looking for.

After a few months, Jackie informed her boss about her actions. She relied on her Narrator and Relationship Deepener strengths to help him understand what she'd been doing in secret. She told her story and had numbers ready to prove that she could sell and develop simultaneously. He laughed and grudgingly gave her permission to continue.

Want another case study?

Jason

Context: Jason had been promoted to supervisor about six months before we began coaching. A bright, ambitious, and compassionate leader with a degree in psychology and an understanding of human nature, Jason was a natural leader. His directs appreciated how he trusted and empowered them to get things done.

Jason's first boss, who had hired him, left the company a year before. The two of them had been very close and fully aligned. After her departure, Jason was instructed to assume a significant portion of her responsibilities. Jason was a bit frustrated by this, since he had initially hoped to be promoted to replace her. Unfortunately, the company decided to eliminate her role. Jason was now doing double duty, managing his current role and carrying out the responsibilities of his former boss.

When I met him, Jason was discouraged and feeling unappreciated. Here he was putting in all this extra effort and not being recognized for it. In his mind, he was performing two roles and was still at a supervisor level. He wanted to be formally recognized for the significant contributions he was making. Money wasn't the issue; he wanted his title to reflect his responsibilities accurately.

His approach to dealing with this was to send an email to his boss and his boss's boss, outlining all the things he was taking on. Unfortunately, he got little or no response from the two leaders above him. Instead, they told him just to do less. Huh? They were the ones who had instructed him to assume these responsibilities.

Jason had to let go of a few things before he could succeed. First and foremost, he had to accept that leadership was no longer about doing, but about relationships. He had taken on so much, thinking that was what would get him noticed (see, I told you this never works), but Jason had neglected to build a solid relationship with his new boss. He was holding on a little too tightly to his desire to have his former boss's job.

When you read further, you'll see that Jason values responsibility. He believed that if he didn't handle these tasks, they'd fall through the cracks and the company would suffer. He was willing to do the work; he just wanted acknowledgement that he was already performing at a high level.

Relationship with supervisor: After his first supervisor left the company, Jason was transferred to a new department with a new boss. While there was evident respect between them, they weren't nearly as sympatico as they could have been. Jason was open to improving this new relationship, however.

Assigned goals: For Jason, being a supervisor meant supervising first and second shift, as well as being responsible for safety on those shifts. Jason's squads were already knocking it out of the proverbial park. So, his assigned goal didn't have anything to do with performance levels.

Instead, Jason's assigned coaching goal was to create greater focus on being a supervisor for his squads, rather than on completing all these other tasks. The thing is, Jason believed he needed to do these different tasks as well.

The motive for keeping it quiet: Jason had received enough pushback to know that what he wanted wasn't necessarily supported by his new boss.

Jason's vision: Jason ultimately wanted recognition and respect. Jason and I had work to do to help him find a clear vision. Eventually, he decided on this: "I am an effective leader, one valued for his contributions, and listened to for his insights and experience."

Rallying cry: "I'm a trusted advisor and leader."

Jason's values:

✓ **Competence:** No matter what, Jason always wanted to be known for doing good, solid work.

✓ **Understanding:** Jason, with his psychology degree, prided himself on understanding the people around him.

✓ **Ambition:** Jason was driven, not just to earn more but to have an impact. He consistently sought out opportunities and acted upon them.

✓ **Respect:** Jason respected his colleagues and wanted to receive the same respect in return from them.

✔ **Responsibility:** Jason held himself to high standards of accountability, and he expected the same from others.

Jason's strengths:

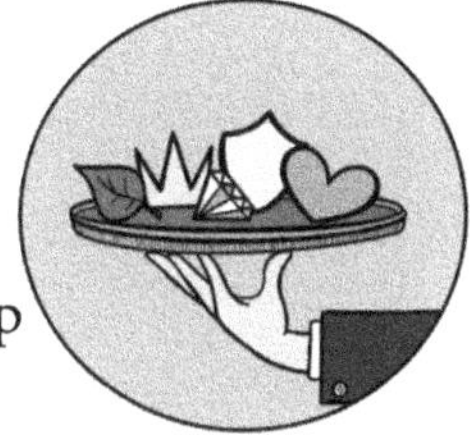

✔ **Work Ethic:** Hard-working, putting a lot of effort into everything.

✔ **Service:** Constantly looking for ways to help and serve others.

✔ **Listening:** Listening intently and focusing on more than what people say, but what they feel too.

✔ **Self-Awareness:** Knowing yourself well and understanding your own emotions and behavior.

✔ **Legacy:** Creating things that will last and delivering a positive and sustainable impact.

JASON'S HIDDEN METRICS

Jason's hidden metrics:

1. Accept that his current approach wasn't working. (Understanding, Respect + Self-Awareness.)

2. Focus on self-satisfaction rather than kudos from others. (Competence, Ambition, Legacy + Work Ethic, Legacy.)

3. Set boundaries. (Respect, Accountability + Work Ethic, Self-Awareness, Listening.)

4. Say, "Yes, and . . ." to requests for assistance. (Competence, Respect, Accountability + Work Ethic, Service, Listening, Self-Awareness.)

5. Resist telling; ask questions of his boss instead. (Understanding, Respect + Listening, Self-Awareness.)

6. Listen more deeply in interacting with his supervisors. (Understanding, Respect, Accountability + Listening, Service, Self-Awareness.)

7. Set priorities rather than reacting to whatever pops up. (Competence, Ambition + Work Ethic, Listening, Legacy.)

Jason's outcome: Jason had an epiphany during our time together. (I love a good epiphany!) He finally came to accept that his current approach of telling his boss—and his boss's boss—about all the extra responsibilities he had taken on was not working. He realized that by taking on these tasks, he thought he was doing a good thing, but he was actually preventing the company from addressing an organizational issue. This was a bigger problem that needed to be addressed through a departmental reorganization. And by continuing to step in, he was allowing leadership to avoid patching that hole.

Jason's epiphany also helped him understand that it was unlikely that anyone would support him the way he expected them to. His judgment about what should happen was getting in the way of reality. That meant he had to accept that he was not getting his former boss's position.

These paradigm shifts helped launch Jason on a new path of self-awareness. He was no longer going to wait for others to give him credit; he would own that responsibility himself. He decided his opinion about his leadership was what mattered most to him. Compliments were still welcome, but Jason freed himself from having to prove himself to others. Instead of pleasing others, he was ready to focus on positive results.

Additionally, Jason was now open to hearing what his boss had to say. What he hadn't realized before was how his boss was showing him a path toward external recognition in this company. Jason had assumed that extra responsibilities and a strong work ethic would get him seen. Simply put, Jason needed to demonstrate he could succeed as a supervisor.

So, the assigned goals were spot on. (It happens sometimes.) That said, Jason still had to find personal meaning in that goal by exploring his vision, value system, and strengths. Instead of being responsible for everything else, Jason shifted his focus to being accountable for himself.

In applying his strengths, Jason realized he was relying too heavily on Work Ethic and Service. At the same time, he was not listening as deeply as he could have to his supervisor. Jason got clear that he needed to utilize Self-Awareness, noticing when his emotions were getting in the way of his relationships. Legacy, as a strength, enabled Jason to focus on demonstrating his best behavior even when feeling discouraged.

Jason also changed his communication style with his superiors. As he listened more carefully, he began to hear what his boss required and how to make it happen.

Jason set boundaries for himself, too, and used "Yes, and . . ." to show his desire to help and then explain why he couldn't.

Ultimately, Jason's vision came true. He became a trusted advisor for his superiors, and he became a leader grounded in his personal values and strengths.

One more case study. I have so many great ones.

Alanna

Context: Alanna is one of those leaders that others want to work for and with: intelligent, optimistic, and skilled. Her promotion to global head of communications occurred a month or two after we started working together. Naturally, this meant creating new goals for herself. Rather than simply leading internal communications, she now had a grander scope and multiple squads.

Alanna was excited about the new position, and she knew things would change for her, but she wasn't quite sure how.

Relationship with supervisor: Fortunately, Alanna had a fantastic relationship with her new supervisor, the CEO. He was a huge fan and was glad to approve her promotion.

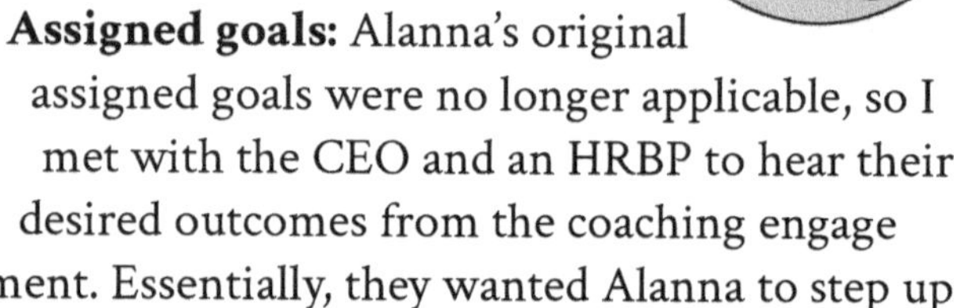

Assigned goals: Alanna's original assigned goals were no longer applicable, so I met with the CEO and an HRBP to hear their desired outcomes from the coaching engage ment. Essentially, they wanted Alanna to step up and be more of an "enterprise leader," not just a squad leader.

The motive for keeping it quiet: Alanna could have shared her hidden metrics with the CEO; he would have understood and been supportive. That said, she was aware of his schedule and the heavy responsibilities he had. She preferred to work on these goals independently.

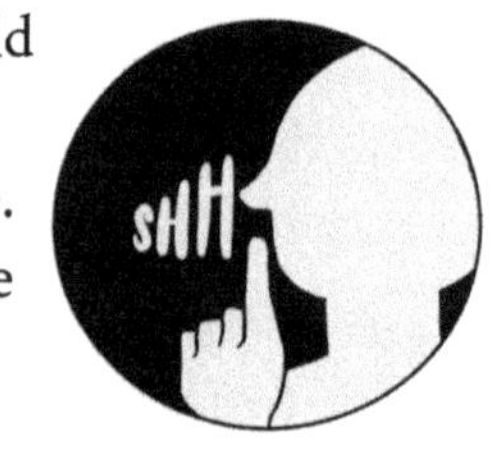

Alanna's vision: "Be an enterprise leader" is somewhat vague, so Alanna defined it as follows: "I am a leader of people and the business." Alanna knew it was essential to be perceived as more than just a communications specialist. At the same time, Alanna understood she was still responsible for her global communications squads. She couldn't ignore or neglect them and focus all her attention on the company. She had to find a balance and succeed at both.

Rallying cry: "Be the mortar, not the brick." This clever phrase perfectly captured her role. As a leader, she was going to hold things together, including her squads and other departments. Her mortar consisted of listening to others, understanding their needs, and making sure everyone succeeds, not just her squads.

Alanna's values:

✔ **Accountability:** Remaining accountable to her squads and to her CEO was essential to Alanna's definition of success that matters.

✔ **Future orientation:** Regularly thinking about the impact of her decisions on the future of the company and her squads was also deeply important.

✔ **Authenticity:** Alanna was herself, no matter where she was or who she was with. It was important to her that whatever she did, it had to reflect her authentic self.

✔ **Service:** Alanna found meaning in being there for others, though she knew she couldn't do that as frequently as she had when she only had one squad to run.

✔ **Inclusion:** Bringing others in to hear their thoughts and recommendations made Alanna's decisions better.

Alanna's strengths:

✔ **Mission:** Pursuing the things that give you a sense of meaning and purpose in life.

✔ **Strategic Awareness:** Paying attention to the broader context and the bigger picture to inform your decisions.

✔ **Unconditionality:** Accepting people for who and what they are without judging them.

✔ **Improving:** Constantly looking for better ways of doing things and gauging how things can be improved.

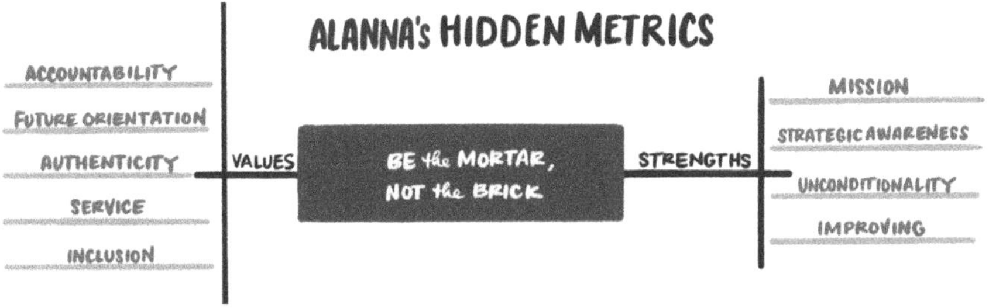

Alanna's hidden metrics:

1. See herself as a business leader. (Accountability, Authenticity + Mission, Strategic Awareness.)

2. Establish regular meetings with key stakeholders and learn what is most important to them. (Future Orientation, Inclusion, Service + Mission, Unconditionality, Improving.)

3. In meetings, look for connections between topics and initiatives. (Future Orientation, Service, Inclusion + Improving, Strategic Awareness.)

4. Set boundaries; step away from meetings that others can handle. (Accountability, Inclusion + Mission, Strategic Awareness, Improving.)

5. Set time to think every week. (Accountability, Future Orientation + Strategic Awareness, Improving.)

6. Challenge the status quo. (Accountability, Future Orientation, Service + Strategic Awareness, Improving.)

7. Demonstrate innovative thinking. (Accountability, Future Orientation, Service + Mission, Strategic Awareness, Improving.)

8. Determine a shared vision for her four squads. (Accountability, Future Orientation, Inclusion + Mission, Strategic Awareness, Unconditionality, Improving.)

9. Empower trusted direct reports to manage meetings and make decisions. (Accountability, Future Orientation, Inclusion + Mission, Strategic Awareness, Improving.)

10. Hold skip-levels on a semi-annual basis to hear from the squad doing the work. (Accountability, Future Orientation, Inclusion + Mission, Unconditionality, Improving.)

Alanna's outcome: Alanna was already a top performer. While she'd been promoted multiple times before, she still found herself challenged by this transition. Like many leaders, she had to learn to let go of her former role and fully embrace her new leadership responsibilities. No more doing; she needed time to step back, adopt a strategic viewpoint, and consider what was possible for her, her squads, and her company.

It wasn't easy for Alanna to let go of doing and embrace reflecting on what was possible. I challenged her to critically review her calendar and identify meetings she could step away from—and who she could entrust to lead them in her absence. It took her a few months, but she was finally able to book quiet time for herself on Fridays to think, to ruminate and plan. She enlisted her assistant in protecting that time slot.

Her values kept her on track. She stuck to her vow of Accountability to her squads, the CEO, and the company. Alanna believed she owed them a Future Orientation—always anticipating what was next, what was possible, and what might go wrong. Service came naturally to Alanna, as did Inclusion and Authenticity.

Alanna found a way to balance being both a leader of people and an enterprise leader. Her hidden metrics helped her narrow her focus so she could be both brick-and-mortar. It didn't always happen in equal parts, but it got easier to switch between them.

Deep down, Alanna understood that some of her goals were time-boxed, but others would be ongoing for years. She relied on her strengths of Mission, Strategic Awareness, and Improving to keep her energized and moving forward.

The Coach's Secret

You have a deep well of potential within you. By getting crystal clear about what you want to create for yourself and others and supporting that compelling vision with your guiding values and energizing strengths, you can fashion a future that is profoundly fulfilling and exciting.

It's time to look beyond the basic goals assigned to you. I invite you to accept the power and agency you have within you to create something meaningful for yourself and your colleagues. It's not always easy, but it is so worth it.

9

THE MOST IMPORTANT RELATIONSHIP

I loved and admired Don Grady, my former supervisor. He could switch seamlessly from being tactical to strategic. He was funny, always cracking jokes. He had a lighthearted spirit that continually sought the bright side of things. For Don, problems were indeed opportunities.

I learned so much from Don—not just that I needed to manage my fear, but also how to be authentic and joyful.

He once shared a story about when he was first starting out as an accountant. His boss called him to his office to correct his behavior.

Seems Don was a bit too jovial; he was clearly having too much fun in the office. This was serious work, being part of a global consulting firm. Don's boss wanted him to be more "professional."

As a young man, just starting his career, Don took his supervisor's feedback to heart. Pretty soon, he was hearing from his colleagues, "Is everything okay with you, Don?" His new demeanor suggested something was wrong. They were worried about him.

After two weeks, Don gave up this more subdued façade. He couldn't do it. His work had started to suffer. He dreaded going to the office. He was starting to lose his spark.

Don decided to ignore his boss's feedback and just be himself. Everything turned around. His output improved, and he enjoyed going to the office again. His boss never brought the feedback up again.

If I had been coaching Don at the time, we would have seen his boss's directive as something that wasn't relevant or accurate. Don's happiness made him a better employee. The feedback given to Don was pure projection and not applicable to him.

Had Don's boss insisted he change his behavior anyway, then perhaps Don would have had an upfront dialog with him about it. They would have had to come to some agreement, tacit or otherwise, about Don's demeanor at work. I can only surmise that his boss figured it out because Don stayed with the firm for over twenty years.

My leadership improved while working with Don. We trusted each other, and I knew I could share anything with him. He never judged. His approach was very coach-like, relying on insightful questions (i.e., "What are you afraid of, Nora?"), and his intuition was grounded in years of experience.

As much as I trusted Don, I didn't share my hidden metrics with him. My vision felt too private to me. And I wanted to know I could grow on my own.

My wish for you is to have someone like Don as your supervisor. The quality of your supervisor has a substantial impact on you and your success. If you're wondering whether to share your hidden metrics with your boss, the following should help you decide.

Your Supervisor's Impact on You

The supervisor-direct report relationship is arguably the most influential factor in an individual's job satisfaction, performance, and career trajectory. This relationship can either unlock your potential or become your biggest obstacle to your achievement— personal and/or professional.

Managers have a significant influence on employee engagement. A 2023 study by the Chartered Management Institute found that 50 percent of employees who are unhappy with their supervisor are likely to leave their job within a year. According to a 2024 survey by Edelman, a global communications firm, when employees feel management doesn't trust them, 57 percent say they do not trust their managers in return. Gallup's research shows that a 70 percent variance in team engagement stems directly from the quality of the manager. When a manager is thriving, so is their squad.

Your supervisor controls many of the levers that determine your daily work experience and long-term career prospects. They influence your access to challenging projects, visibility with senior leadership, learning opportunities, and resource allocation. A supportive boss can accelerate your growth by providing stretch assignments, advocating for your promotion, and connecting you with important stakeholders.

On the other hand, a poor manager can stunt your development, create unnecessary stress, and limit your opportunities regardless of your capabilities.

Your relationship with your manager has a significant impact on your willingness to take risks, share ideas, and admit when you need help. When your supervisor has your best interests in mind, you're more likely to be innovative and take on challenges that drive growth. A great manager also understands what inspires you as a person and creates conditions that enable you to do your best work. We all want to feel a sense of psychological safety with our bosses, just as I did with Don.

Remember, too, that this sense of safety flows both ways.

Ultimately, what both you and your leader want is to be able to trust each other.

Creating Trust

Understanding what trust is will help you deepen your trustworthiness and establish a trusting relationship with your colleagues and leader.

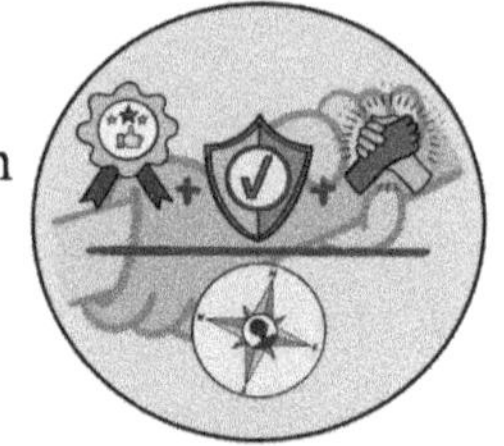

There are several definitions for trust. I use two because not every trust model resonates with every client.

Charles Feltman, executive coach and author of *The Thin Book of Trust*, defines trust as "choosing to risk making something you value vulnerable to another person's actions."

Such a powerful statement. Whether you are handing off a project, presentation, or information, you are choosing to allow someone else to care for it on your behalf. It's no surprise it is scary to trust people at work. You are asking them to watch over something you find essential, important, and valuable to you and your career.

When was the last time you entrusted something personally or professionally valuable to someone else? How did you feel? Were you worried or confident they would do right by you? Did you feel hesitant to hand it off? Or were you eager to let it go?

Anytime you delegate or ask for help, you are relying on someone to be as careful as you would be. That is trust in action.

The Trust Equation

Let's break trust down a bit further with another model from former Harvard professor David Maister and consultant Charles H. Green, from their book *The Trusted Advisor*, called the Trust Equation. The authors created a simple way to identify and explain the key elements of trustworthiness, something we all want to possess.

The trust equation begins with credibility. Is the person you are enlisting to help you knowledgeable, skilled, and capable? Do you believe them to be adept at the task? Will they use good judgment?

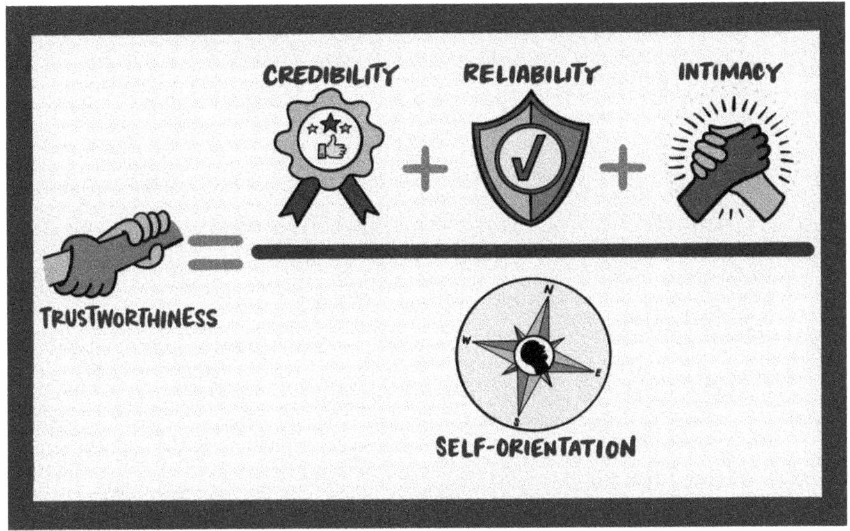

The Trust Equation

Can they deliver what they promise?

Reliability addresses whether the person you want to trust is consistent and able to deliver on time, as planned. Do they have a track record of following through on promises and commitments? Can we predict how they'll behave over a period of time?

Intimacy is a word rarely used in work settings (like Love), but here is how the authors define it. Intimacy is the security and safety others feel when sharing their personal thoughts, feelings, and vulnerabilities, trusting that the information will be handled with confidentiality and discretion. If we hold a high level of intimacy then others will feel emotionally secure enough with us to be vulnerable and transparent, knowing that anything they reveal will be handled respectfully by us.

Finally, Maister and Green add a fourth element to the equation, self-orientation. Essentially, this quality asks you to assess whether the person you want to trust is focused on their needs, goals, or reputation or on you and what you need from them? Are they a team player or just in it for themself?

What is critical to note here is that, regardless of a person's strength in credibility, reliability, and intimacy, if they are highly self-oriented, trust will be that much harder to achieve.

We can assign numbers to the trust equation. In case you feel the need, here's a suggested approach:

Rate each component on a scale of one to ten. Then, use these ratings in the equation to get a Trust Quotient. For example, if you assess someone's trustworthiness on a scale of 1-10, 1 being weak and 10 being strong, you may come up with something like this:

✓ Credibility = 8

✓ Reliability = 7

✓ Intimacy = 5

✓ Self-Orientation = 8

The Trust Quotient would be $(8 + 7 + 5) / 8 = 2.25$. This would be considered a low value and undesirable. Remember, a high score in self-orientation indicates they are centered on what they want or think they need. They don't care as much about anyone else. You can see how a high self-orientation rating has an inverse relationship on the overall trustworthiness of this person. No matter how you score someone on the other elements, if they are focused primarily on themselves, it will be difficult to create lasting trust.

Here's another example:

✓ Credibility = 8

✓ Reliability = 3

✓ Intimacy = 7

✓ Self-Orientation = 2

This person knows what they are doing, but they may not deliver when and how as expected. They may also be open, authentic and focused on the success of the team. Their quotient would be: $(8 + 3 + 7) / 2 = 9$, a high trust score. You may want to have a conversation with this person and see what they can do to be on time and more reliable, but generally, they are trustworthy.

Rather than using numerical ratings, I prefer to take a different tack in working with the Trust Equation. Not surprisingly, since I'm a coach, I'll ask questions to gauge someone's trustworthiness.

Credibility: Level of expertise, knowledge, and competence

✔ Does this person know how to do what I'm asking?

✔ Will this be a stretch goal for them?

✔ What might be missing that they'll need help with?

✔ Have I asked them to do something similar in the past that worked well for them?

✔ If they failed in the past, have they learned from their mistakes?

Reliability: Consistent delivery of what's been promised

✔ Does this person deliver on time?

✔ Do they deliver what I asked them to do?

✔ If not, what systems or help do they need to become more reliable?

Intimacy: Discreet, empathetic, safe

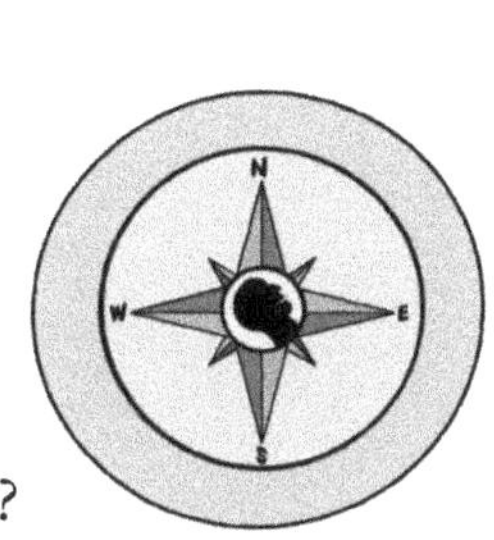

✔ Has this person kept confidences in the past?

✔ Do they understand the risk and importance of what I'm asking them to do?

✔ Do I feel safe sharing my thoughts and feelings with them?

Self-Orientation: In it for themself

✔ What is the motivation for this person to assist me?

✔ Have they demonstrated their desire to advance team goals?

✔ How often do they share credit with others?

✔ Do they use "I" more often than "we" when talking about their accomplishments?

As you become accustomed to using the Trust Equation, I invite you to assess not only the trustworthiness of others but also your own. Be rigorous in evaluating yourself. There may be ways in which you can improve your own level of trustworthiness.

Repairing Trust

Most people seem to view trust as an on/off switch: Either you have it, or you don't. When it is in the off position, it can feel too heavy and difficult to try to get it back into the on position. Repairing trust takes time and effort,  but it is possible to patch it up enough to make the relationship work. The Trust Equation is a great starting point for planning to repair trust once it has been damaged.

For example, if you judge a co-worker to be highly credible and intimate, low on self-orientation, but not reliable, then you have some clarity about how far you can trust them. From your vantage point, you know they'll do a fine job, but they will likely deliver late, after the deadline. With this information, you can plan to have a conversation about how to remedy this and improve your levels of trust.

In your conversation, you might begin by saying, "Thank you for agreeing to help me with strategic planning. I know you'll deliver exactly what we need. I'm concerned, though, that I've seen a pattern in how you miss deadlines. What can you do to make sure you'll submit your report when we need it?"

Notice I didn't say anything about whether I trust this person. Telling someone you don't trust them is bound to trigger a defensive reaction. That's not what you want. Build trust, don't tear it down.

You might also notice in the example that I didn't tell the person how to fix the problem. To get their buy-in, let them come up with the solution.

Let's try a more challenging example, one based on a real client.

I coached Max, a senior director, on his leadership skills. I assessed him as highly credible, reliable, and intimate. While every single coaching conversation ever held is laser-focused on the coachee, I sensed that Max was primarily interested in his own triumphs not those of his squad or the company; he had a high level of self-orientation.

As part of our coaching agreement, I agreed to conduct a 360-degree assessment on Max. This involved creating an interview protocol, conducting in-person interviews, and capturing responses from Max's peers, directs, and supervisors.

From his peers, I learned that Max spent a lot of time entertaining his bosses and senior leadership. They all spoke glowingly of Max; he was a great, fun guy. They loved hanging out with him.

That was one viewpoint. Unfortunately, in other interviews, I learned that his squad hesitated to go to him for advice and help. They didn't trust him.

In addition, as Max and I discussed what he wanted to achieve through coaching, his comments centered on how he could persuade his squad to do what he wanted.

This is an important distinction. Max wasn't requesting that I help him inspire or even motivate his squad. He didn't ask how to be a better leader. He didn't want to know how to apply their strengths more constructively. No, Max was more interested in controlling and manipulating.

I'm afraid Max was the kind of toxic leader who courts senior leadership and disciplines those lower on the career ladder. His philosophy was "kiss up kick down." (Not something you'll find on my Hidden Metrics Values List.) Max spent a lot of effort on impression management, ensuring he presented himself well to the higher-ups. This was a bright red flag, suggesting he had a high level of self-orientation.

It's my job as a coach to share this feedback, so I confronted Max about his pattern of behavior and used the Trust Equation to help me.

Together, we walked through the 360-degree feedback, which revealed how his peers and supervisors enjoyed working with him and trusted him to do quality work, on time (intimacy, credibility, reliability). He appreciated hearing this.

Then I shared how respondents said he had created a reputation for being only concerned with himself and his victories (self-orientation). Bound by confidentiality agreements, I could only share, at a high level, the patterns people were seeing in his behavior.

To be clear, I didn't present the Trust Equation model to Max during our meeting. I did use it to guide the delivery of the feedback, however.

Max disagreed with the comments. He insisted he was there to make the company successful; he just had a squad that needed a lot of direction.

I asked him to pause and consider why others might have this impression of him. Was there anything he had done in the past that would make him look like he was only in it for himself? Could he explain why so many people saw him this way? Could he offer up examples of how he gave credit to others, celebrated a job well done, or supported someone else even though it may have cost him to do so? His replies felt weak and incomplete.

Coaches often have difficult conversations with their clients. Eventually, we become comfortable with direct communication, but it is rarely easy. I wasn't looking forward to sharing the results of his 360 with Max, but I did. I don't expect you to enjoy it either; however, sometimes these tough conversations are worth it because repairing trust is worth it. You can do the same using Maister's Trust Equation as a framework. I was hopeful Max would realize how he was damaging trust at all levels. His squad didn't trust him, and senior leadership would eventually learn that he was manipulating them too.

I would love to write a positive epilogue to Max's story, a happy ending. Unfortunately, it didn't turn out that way. It would give you a false belief that having one conversation is enough. Sometimes, multiple conversations are required. And sometimes people choose not to change.

Max chose not to change. He was soon dismissed from the company, but not because of how he treated his direct reports. He was fired for ethics violations.

Trust and Your Supervisor

If you want to share your hidden metrics with your supervisor, consider your relationship with them first. Trust flows both ways, after all. Supervisors need to trust their direct reports to deliver and make good decisions, while directs need to trust that their manager will support them, provide honest feedback, and advocate for their interests. This trust is built over time.

How would you gauge your levels of trust with each other?

Both parties need to understand priorities, expectations, team goals, and boundaries. Regular one-on-ones should focus not just on status updates but on obstacles, career development, and alignment. Great leaders are explicit about what success looks like and provide context for why certain work matters.

If you find that you are not on the same page as your supervisor, it's up to you to be proactive and request what you need. Let your boss know that you'd like to structure your one-on-ones so you can gain a deeper understanding of their vision and what they need to make it a reality.

While maintaining a professional demeanor, the best supervisor-direct report relationships involve genuine care for each other as people. This means understanding what's happening in each other's lives, celebrating successes together, and providing support during difficult times. This human connection creates loyalty and makes work more fulfilling. (Remember these connections make work meaningful.)

Are your interactions with your boss limited to dry, status-driven discussions? It's on you to switch it up. Start asking questions and learn who your supervisor is as a person, not just a boss.

Rarely does a supervisor reject sincere questions or put up walls. However, I have had former clients tell me they prefer not to disclose much about their personal lives at work, especially to their direct reports. They worry about crossing boundaries or sending mixed messages. Other supervisors may need more time before they feel comfortable sharing details. Ultimately, some supervisors remain closed off. That doesn't mean you can't share what's going on in your life; in fact, you should. Learn to accept that your boss may not score as highly as you on the Trust Equation Intimacy scale.

With time, your relationship with your reticent boss will grow. As you build trust (and repair it quickly when it's damaged), you can create an authentic and truthful partnership.

The best supervisors provide context and feedback to help you understand how your work fits into the bigger picture. Regular, quality feedback enables you to course-correct quickly rather than discovering problems during formal reviews. Great managers also help you identify blind spots and develop skills you might not recognize you need. This ongoing dialogue is essential for continuous improvement and building confidence for both of you.

If you aren't getting actionable feedback from your supervisor, ask for it. Your career is your responsibility, so take the initiative. When you do request input, instead of posing the question as "How am I doing?" be more specific. Ask, "What are your thoughts about how I conducted the recent strategy meeting? What could I do better? How could I have encouraged people to get more involved? How could I improve on how I answered their questions?" Being more precise in your queries will enable your supervisor to give you more specific comments.

If you have a stellar boss, like Don, they will see developing their people as a core responsibility, not an extra task. This means understanding your career goals, providing relevant learning opportunities, and helping you build skills that serve both your current needs and future aspirations.

If you require additional development, seek it out and inform your supervisor. It may involve enrolling in a training program that will enhance your leadership skills. Maybe you would like to get to know their peers better. Ask your boss to facilitate an introduction so you can meet and learn about them. If you hear about a company-wide initiative, discuss with your supervisor whether you can participate in it.

Repairing Trust with Your Supervisor

If you feel that trust has been damaged in your relationship with your boss, take the bold step and have the tough conversation about what you both need to succeed. Take Lucy, for example.

Lucy enjoyed working with her boss, Terry, for the most part. However, Lucy noticed that Terry seemed to change his mind frequently. Terry would agree on a direction but then move in the opposite direction in the next meeting. Lucy was starting to feel as though she couldn't count on Terry's word anymore. Trust was damaged.

This is how Lucy prepared to have a conversation about trust with Terry:

✔ Lucy began by writing down the specifics of when Terry's messaging shifted.

✔ Lucy then focused on a common goal. What is it that she and Terry were working toward? Lucy didn't feel she could serve their internal customers well if the plans kept changing, and Terry had already declared that their internal customers were their number one priority.

✔ Selecting a day, time, and location for the meeting, Lucy made sure they wouldn't be interrupted and that they could speak openly in private.

Once the meeting began:

✔ Lucy spoke honestly about how she appreciated Terry's leadership. She also noted that she wanted to make sure she was still aligned with Terry's vision and planning. "I'd like to discuss some communication patterns that have confused me lately."

✔ Rather than running through each example, Lucy discussed the pattern of behavior she observed and its impact on her and her customer group. "I know meeting their needs is essential to our success."

✔ Lucy prepared for possible responses from Terry. If Terry got defensive, Lucy would stay calm and focus on how to work better in the future. If Terry denied or minimized the issue, Lucy would be ready to share an example if needed, but she wasn't going to get pulled into a debate. She would keep a focus on how to work together in the future.

✔ As Lucy talked with Terry, she kept in mind that Terry, like everyone else, was doing the best he could. Lucy wanted to solve the problem, not accuse or blame.

✔ To end the meeting, Lucy summarized their agreements.

Lucy entered the meeting with a noble intent, assuming that everyone was doing their best. With this attitude, the likelihood of Terry saying anything wrong was diminished. The assumptions we make and the emotions we hold directly affect our tone and vocabulary. If Lucy had entered the room with a chip on her shoulder feeling resentful, the conversation would have gone in a completely different direction. Instead, it turned out to be a great discussion that resulted in clear action steps.

Lucy also had gone into the meeting acknowledging that she could improve too. She committed to remaining open to any feedback Terry had for her.

Lucy learned that Terry was feeling overwhelmed and was having a hard time tracking the decisions he had been making. Terry's boss would sometimes push for a different choice, and Terry wanted to support him. Lucy walked away with a better understanding of what was happening in the background, empathy for what Terry was going through, and a plan for how to support each other as they moved forward.

Most importantly, trust between these two was repaired. Had Lucy not said anything, her resentment would have increased, and their relationship could have gotten worse.

Sharing Your Hidden Metrics Safely

If you decide to share your hidden metrics with your boss and/or HRBP, there are a few things to keep in mind.

✓ Determine how well you trust them before you share your metrics. If you sense they are not entirely in your corner, you should reconsider.

✓ Your boss wants to see you make progress toward the assigned goals. So do your best to phrase your hidden metrics so it's clear each one is designed to support your plan to hit the goals they specified. We aren't forgetting them. We are approaching them in a way that works best for you.

✓ Ask them to keep it confidential. Explain that you are trying new things and would like to be able to try without the extra weight of other people's opinions and expectations.

✓ Enlist your boss and HR in supporting you as you work toward your hidden metrics. Ask them to let you know when they catch you doing something great.

Your supervisors can be assets on your journey of growth and development, but only if you have relationships built on trust and understanding.

The Coach's Secret

Professional coaches will tell you that the most important relationship you have at work is with your immediate supervisor. Finding time to connect, especially if you work in different locations, is essential for you to trust them and for them to trust you. Be curious about who they are as people not just as what their titles might imply.

If you are lucky enough to have a supportive, empathetic, and wise boss (like Don Grady), feel free to share your hidden metrics with them. If you determine that the mutual trustworthiness is not where it could be, give yourself permission to keep your hidden metrics private.

The relationship between you and your supervisor requires effort from both sides, but when it works well, it becomes a powerful engine for individual growth and meaningful achievements.Oh, by the way, I lied.

There is another relationship to be mindful of . . .

10
AN EVEN MORE IMPORTANT RELATIONSHIP

That other relationship to be mindful of? The one with yourself. You are the most important relationship you have.

Creating hidden metrics is only one way to honor who you truly are, to respect the values and strengths you carry with you every day. You are a marvelous and unique miracle, and every miracle deserves to be celebrated.

Most of us, though, don't see ourselves that way. Most days, I don't. When my coaching is effective or I write a particularly clear sentence or I make someone smile, I might remember that I'm one of a kind. But mostly, I see myself as a flawed human just trying to make do. My relationship with myself could improve.

The kind of relationship you have with yourself is more important than the relationship you have with your boss. Just like Beyoncé says, "Your self-worth is determined by you." Your superior may think you are brilliant, but if you don't see that light within yourself, you'll never believe them when they compliment you.

What's Your Archetype?

How you perceive yourself directly impacts your version of success. Rajiv viewed himself as beneath senior leadership. As long as he held onto that self-perception, he wasn't going to grow. Rajiv saw himself as just a regular guy doing his work—an Everyman—certainly not as a leader of leaders.

The Everyman is an archetype, just like the Leader. Archetypes can be used to help us describe how we are and imagine how we want to be. Essentially, an archetype is a universal pattern or image that exists in the collective unconscious of humanity. For example, when I mention the archetype of "Rock Star," we all immediately conjure up a similar vision of what that means: a passionate, rocking musician at the top of their game. Archetypes give us a shorthand way to communicate images, concepts, and behaviors.

Carl Jung, a ground-breaking psychoanalyst from the early twentieth century, developed the concept of archetypes. He saw them as innate inclinations that shape how we perceive, experience, and respond to life. To Jung, they represent the deepest layer of unconscious material that all humans share. Because archetypes are so deeply ingrained, we might not even notice them.

Key Characteristics of Archetypes

Archetypes show up as recurring themes, symbols, and character types that appear consistently across cultures, mythologies, literature, and individual dreams and fantasies. For example, Luke Skywalker and Harry Potter exemplify the Hero/Achiever archetype; Obi-Wan Kenobi and Professor Dumbledore, the Mentor/Sage. There are many other archetypes including fun ones like, "Rock Star" or "Playful Child." Some depict stages of growth, like "Knight," "Lover," or "King," or "Maiden," "Mother", or "Crone." In her book *Sacred Contracts*, best-selling author Carolyn Myss describes over seventy different archetypes.

By their very nature, archetypes carry enormous emotional energy and psychological power. When we activate them in our lives, they can profoundly influence our behavior, relationships, and sense of meaning. They often emerge during significant life transitions or intense experiences. They provide templates to help us understand life's fundamental patterns and challenges.

Here are a few of the most common archetypes seen at work:

✔ **The Leader/Ruler** embodies authority and takes charge of situations. These individuals naturally assume responsibility, make decisions confidently, and work to establish order and direction within teams or organizations. (My client Eric, for sure, fits here. Nice guy, focused on doing the right thing. Not as effective as he could have been. He challenged himself and became a stronger, more influential leader. These days, Eric embodies the Leader/Ruler archetype.)

✔ **The Mentor/Sage** serves as a wise advisor who shares knowledge and guides the development of others. They're often sought out for their experience and insight, helping colleagues navigate challenges and grow professionally. (My former boss Don is a perfect example of the Mentor/Sage.)

✓ **The Innovator/Creator** brings fresh ideas and creative solutions to problems. They thrive on developing new approaches, challenging conventional thinking, and finding novel ways to improve processes or products. (No doubt Steve Jobs fits the bill.)

✓ **The Caregiver/Nurturer** focuses on supporting squad members and maintaining group harmony. They're attentive to others' needs, offer emotional support, and strive to create inclusive and comfortable work environments. (Maria Shriver fits well here. She helped care for her father who had Alzheimer's and later founded the Women's Alzheimer's Movement.)

✓ **The Rebel/Revolutionary** challenges existing systems and pushes for change. They question established procedures, advocate for improvements, and aren't afraid to disrupt the status quo when they believe transformation is needed. (Gloria Steinem, journalist and social activist, is an perfect example of the Rebel/Revolutionary.)

✓ **The Hero/Achiever** takes on complex challenges and strives to overcome obstacles. They're driven by accomplishment, willing to make sacrifices to win, and often step up during crises or high-pressure situations. (A conductor on the Underground Railroad, Harriet Tubman exemplifies the Hero/Achiever. She repeatedly risked her own life to guide hundreds of enslaved people to freedom.)

✓ **The Explorer/Seeker** pursues new opportunities and ventures into uncharted territory. They're comfortable with ambiguity, enjoy discovering possibilities, and often drive expansion or exploration of new markets or ideas. (Amelia Earhart refused to allow traditional barriers stop her from doing what she felt she was meant to do.)

✔ **The Jester/Entertainer** brings lightness and humor to the workplace. They help relieve tension, boost morale, and create positive energy, although they may sometimes struggle to be taken seriously in matters of importance. (Jim Carrey fits here.)

✔ **The Loyal Supporter/Everyman** provides a steady and reliable contribution, valuing team cohesion. They're dependable, collaborative, and work to maintain group stability and shared purpose. (President Jimmy Carter was a peanut farmer before he ran for office. Even after he departed the White House, he continued his role as a Loyal Supporter/Everyman through his work with Habitat for Humanity.)

Which one(s) resonate most with you?

The Victim Archetype

There is one archetype that we all experience at some point in our lives: the Victim. The Victim emerges when we feel powerless and overwhelmed by things beyond our control. It can encompasses both the genuine experience of being victimized and past patterns of learned helplessness.

We dislike seeing ourselves as a Victim, but there are times when we are. At its core, the Victim experiences life as something that happens to them rather than something they can shape and construct. Victims will often feel at the mercy of circumstances or other people's decisions. They do not believe they have the agency to turn things around. They may feel betrayed, abandoned, abused, or indignant. Because of these feelings, Victims want to be rescued, desperately.

As you consider your current work situation and your new role, ask yourself whether you feel a little bit Victim-y. Perhaps the announcement of your promotion didn't go as planned, and you feel you must defend why you have been elevated to this role.

Or, you have been assigned a squad of unskilled players who are going to struggle getting anywhere near your goals, let alone hit them. Or maybe you have a supervisor who neglects you, leaving you to fend for yourself. Those situations might prompt any of us to adopt the Victim archetype.

The thing is, when you move into Victim, you may trigger others to take on less-than-desirable archetypes as they interact with you. Let me introduce you to the Drama Triangle.

The Drama Triangle

In coaching circles, we sometimes refer to the Karpman Drama Triangle. First presented in 1968 by psychiatrist Stephen B. Karpman, MD, and later thoroughly covered in his landmark 2014 book, *A Game Free Life: The New Transactional Analysis of Intimacy, Openness, and Happiness*, this model depicts the dysfunction between a Victim, Persecutor, and Rescuer. These three archetypes appear in the workplace fairly frequently, and they have one thing in common: they occur when actors are fixated on what they *don't* want.

Let's say you are upset with your boss because he hasn't gotten you the resources you need to be successful. So, you go to him, and he tells you, "No, no more staff. Budgets are tight!" Plus, he snarkily adds that you should be able to hit your goals without extra help. After all, when he was in your position, he was able to pull it off. After this conversation, you feel inadequate and even a little persecuted. He's no help, so you go to seek solace with someone else, one of your boss's peers. She listens and agrees to step in and rescue you. She's going to run interference and talk to your boss on your behalf. You feel better because the problem is now off your shoulders.

A frequent scenario, though not a healthy one.

In this situation, you took on the role of the Victim. You felt powerless, hopeless, oppressed, and eager to blame someone or something. Your boss was the ideal target. He wasn't helpful, just insulting. Why was he treating you this way?

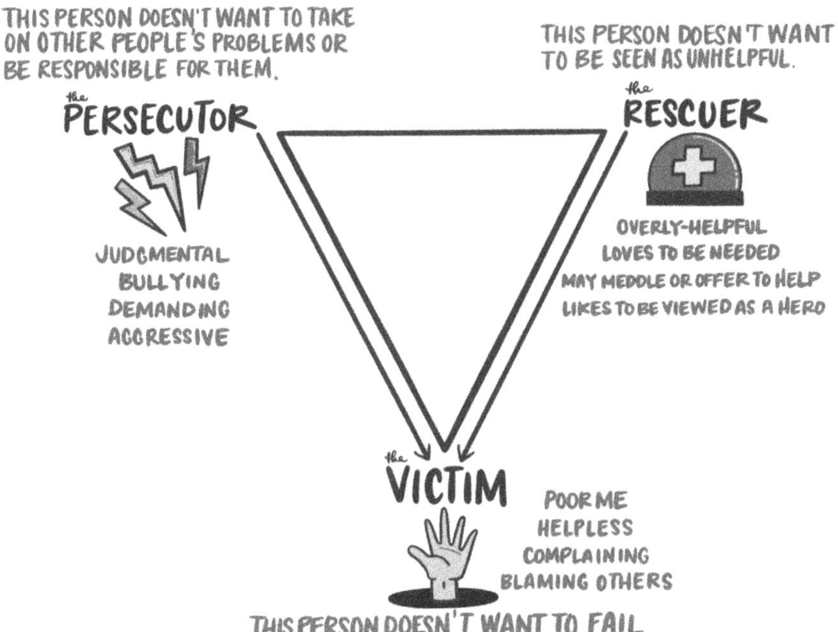

The Drama Triangle

While you were being a Victim, your boss reacted by taking on the archetype of the Persecutor. He became rigid, defensive, and superior. He set standards based on his own work experience. He judged you and held you accountable.

The Rescuer loved that you came to her. She enjoyed running interference and putting her nose where it doesn't belong. She liked being known as a savior or hero and would do what she could to help you, relieving you of any responsibility to repair the situation. Also, she'd rather help you than deal with all her own responsibilities. She could handle those later.

The Drama Triangle demonstrates unhealthy, passive, and ineffective behaviors. Do you remember how I mentioned earlier on that when creating hidden metrics, we need to focus on what we do want, not what we don't want? It's the same principle in the Drama Triangle. Each participant is acting from a clear understanding of what they don't want, not what they do.

You, as the Victim, don't want to fail or to have to beg for resources. The Persecutor, your supervisor, doesn't want the risk associated with a failed project. He also doesn't want to spend the time and energy needed to help you—someone he has already judged to be incapable. Finally, the Rescuer doesn't want her self-image to be destroyed. She doesn't want to feel guilty about letting someone handle this on their own. She also would rather not concentrate on her own projects. The Rescuer might be so busy helping others that she doesn't get her work done. (Remember how we covered saying yes to special requests too frequently? Being a savior works against the Rescuer because she is not paying enough attention to her own responsibilities.)

In the Drama Triangle, the players often avoid taking responsibility for truly improving or challenging themselves to become better.

When we only attend to what we don't want, we run the risk of taking on one of these unhealthy archetypes. What's worse is that we end up with more of what we don't want. Because our attention is dedicated to avoiding the undesirable, we inadvertently create more of it.

All those years ago, when I was freaking out because someone didn't deliver when I asked them to, I was playing the Victim. And as I was yelling and swearing, I was playing the role of the Persecutor. Part of me wishes there had been a Rescuer, but there wasn't. What I really needed was a different way of relating to myself.

The Empowerment Triangle

In the Drama Triangle, your relationship with yourself is ineffective and unempowering. You may not refer to yourself as a Victim, but you are behaving as one. What if there were another way to relate to ourselves in those kinds of situations? There is! It's called the Empowerment Triangle, developed by David Emerald Womeldorff. His book, *The Power of TED** demonstrates how we can reclaim our power.

Essentially, the Drama Triangle can be flipped on its head to become the Empowerment Triangle by encouraging each player to start thinking about what they sincerely do want.

152

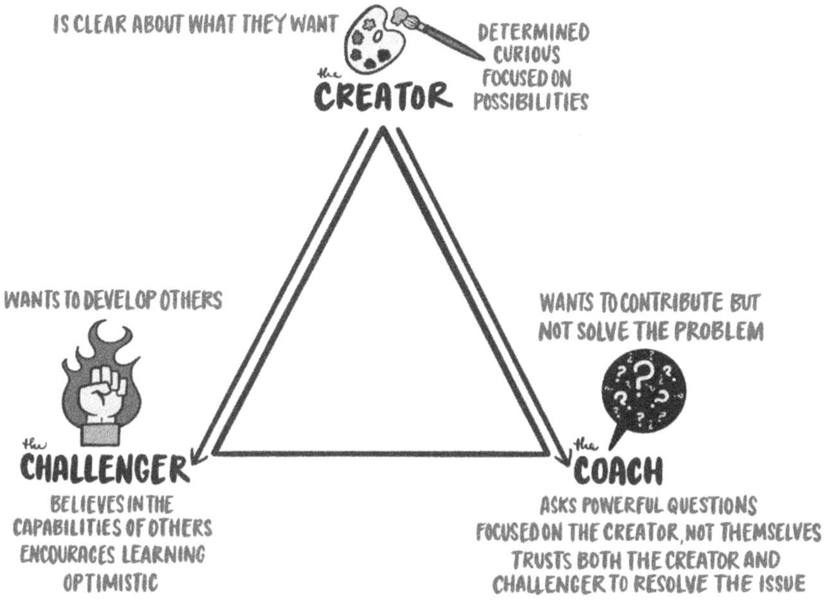

The Empowerment Dynamic

Instead of the Victim archetype, you take on the Creator archetype: someone who owns their competence and power. The Creator refuses to take the issue personally and instead zeroes in on finding a solution. Rather than whining "poor me," their mantra is "I can find a solution." The Creator knows what they want: to figure it out, to achieve the goal, to challenge themself, and to grow. They go to their boss to get insights, direction—not to be saved.

Now think about this. If you approach your supervisor in a confident, curious, Creator-like way, they will instinctively interact with you differently.

If you do, then the Persecutor is free to take on the Challenger archetype. In this more positive state of mind, the Challenger encourages the Creator. Instead of diminishing you, the Challenger reassures you and says, "I know you can do this." They embolden the Creator to learn more, maybe pointing them in the right direction to a key subject matter expert. Or perhaps they willingly brainstorm new possibilities with the Creator. The Challenger wants to develop their direct report and to prove to them that they have what it takes to succeed.

Finally, the Rescuer converts to Coach. The Coach supports and assists the Creator by asking questions, such as, "What have you done so far?" "What is a simple first step you can take?" and "What is the bold move you want to make?" The Coach doesn't run interference or represent the Creator in any way. The Coach wants to encourage and question and then they go back to completing their own work.

Hidden Metrics and You, as Creator

As you think about your relationship with yourself, reflect on how and when you show up as a Victim. When do you feel that sense of powerlessness or lack of hope? What is going on in those situations? How can you shift yourself away from being a Victim to being a Creator?

If you've begun to create your vision, you have already made the move toward shaping your future. That's because you've already checked in with your ideal self, your intuition, and you know what it is you *want*. In creating your hidden metrics, you are already using the Creator archetype.

Creators are outcome-focused. They are confident they can manifest their vision. They carry a naturally optimistic attitude with them, which becomes contagious as they work with others. Creators hold a basic assumption: They have the agency to build their own lives. Things do not happen to them; they have the power to make things happen.

How can you make sure you act from the Creator archetype more frequently than the Victim? Here are some practices to adopt that will help you make the mental, emotional, and physical shift to being a Creator.

Creator Practices

For your hidden metrics to work, learn how to appreciate yourself and your gifts and adopt the Creator archetype. Here are some suggestions. Like anything, the more frequently you practice these things, the more they will be internalized.

✓ **Practice self-awareness**: Regularly check in with your thoughts, feelings, and reactions without judgment. That judgment piece can be tricky. Here's a coaching tip: Imagine yourself on a balcony, looking down upon yourself as you interact with others or even while you are alone. From your metaphorical balcony, what do you see? This approach helps you detach emotionally from whatever is happening and enables you to observe yourself from a higher, more objective perspective. You might also want to journal, meditate, or simply pause throughout the day to notice what's happening internally.

✓ **Listen to your body/language/emotions:** When you are feeling defeated or Victim-like, your body, language, and emotions will send you cues, like slumped shoulders and low energy. You may shake your head a lot. Your language will sound defeated or resigned: "It won't work. I've tried everything." You might even try to invite others to listen to your sad story and agree that, yes, you are getting a bad deal. Sometimes the attention feels nice. Ultimately, you will feel sad, lost, disempowered, and fatalistic. When you notice these cues, pause and make a deliberate shift. Find an inspiring quote, play a favorite song, dance, get outside or call a friend. Shake it off!

✓ **Develop self-compassion:** Treat yourself with the same kindness you'd show a good friend. When you make mistakes or face challenges, avoid harsh self-criticism and instead offer yourself understanding and encouragement. You are doing your best, and if you are like most of my clients, your best, even on your off days, is spectacular. Find an old childhood photo of yourself. Put it on your desk. Remind yourself that underneath it all, you are still just that little kid. Show a little compassion to the tyke that you still are.

✓ **Test yourself:** There's a concept coaches call "self-efficacy." It's the belief that you can successfully perform actions needed to manage future situations. When you ask yourself, "Can I do this?" and you respond by saying, "Yes, I can do this," you have created a powerful act of self-affirmation. By consciously asserting your belief in yourself and your capabilities, you tap into your innate potential and are better able to navigate challenges with greater confidence and resilience. So, ask yourself, "Can I do this?"

✓ **Honor your values and boundaries:** Identify what truly matters to you and make choices that align with those principles. This includes saying no to things that drain you and yes to what energizes and fulfills you. Use your strengths to keep you going and your values to keep on track.

✓ **Engage in regular self-care:** This means attending to your physical, emotional, mental, and spiritual needs in ways that go beyond surface-level activities, in a manner that feels genuine and restorative to you. It does not mean scheduling a massage every once in a while. Self-care only works to support us and keep us healthy and balanced if we make it a daily practice. Take a walk, sit in the grass, call a friend, read a book, drink some water.

✓ **Listen to your ideal self:** Pay attention to what your body and emotions are telling you about situations, relationships, and decisions, and trust your intuition. Listen to the stories you tell yourself and decide if your ego is telling you the truth.

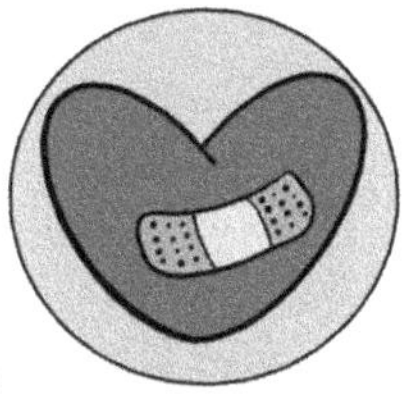

✔ **Forgive others and yourself:** Move past mistakes and work on healing old wounds. This might involve therapy, creative expression, or other forms of processing and growth. There is nothing more liberating than forgiving others and oneself. Remind yourself that everyone is doing what they can with what they have, including you.

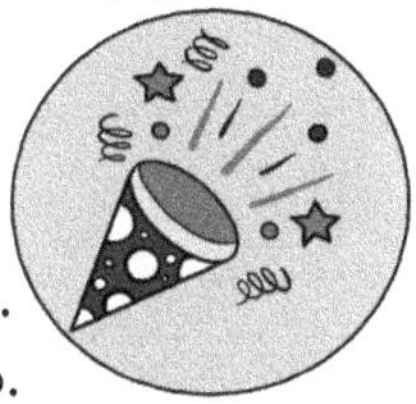

✔ **Celebrate your strengths and progress:** Acknowledge your accomplishments, both big and small, and recognize how far you've come, while also accepting your imperfections. This is something my clients say they rarely do. Instead, they move from one accomplishment to another without a break, taking no time to recognize what just happened. Take the time to acknowledge all the threads that had to come together to make something—anything—happen.

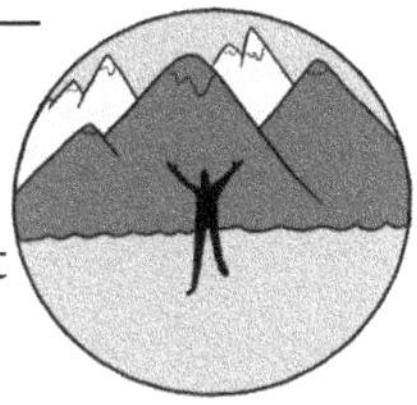

✔ **Create space for solitude:** Be with yourself without distractions. This helps you reconnect with who you are beneath all the roles and responsibilities.

The Coach's Secret

As you begin to implement your hidden metrics, you will be tempted to be self-critical about your progress. Some things will be easy, while others will be a stretch. Cut yourself some slack as you grow. Trust your ideal self, your intuition, your experience, and your knowledge. Like Dorothy from *The Wizard of Oz,* you have everything you need to get where you want to go. The relationship with yourself is ongoing and ever evolving. Be patient with the process and remember that self-love is a practice, not a destination.

We've covered a lot so far. But you may still have one large question looming in the back of your mind: What if . . . it doesn't work?

11
WHAT IF IT DOESN'T WORK?

What happens if you follow the midden metrics equation—you define your vision, name your values, apply your strengths, write down your hidden metrics, and work diligently to achieve them—and then you realize it's not working? What if your company won't support you in creating your future? What if your boss works against you or, at the very least, isn't supportive? What if all your effort is showing you don't belong there? What if you now realize the company culture is wrong for you?

What do you do?

Do you resign? Do you go along to get along? Do you deny your ideal self its chance to run free?

Do you rework your hidden metrics? Maybe you had the wrong vision? Perhaps you made a mistake along the way?

These are big questions and not something any coach can answer for you. I can, however, provide you with additional points to consider as you figure it out.

My First Coaching Gig

My very first coaching engagement (eons ago) was with a marketing team for a large multi-national company. I booked the entire team— twenty-four people! I quickly learned this department had suffered through four departmental reorganizations in three years. This group of souls was exhausted, demoralized, and ready to jump ship.

Twenty-two of the twenty-four told me in our very first meetings that they planned to leave. Each shared a story of how hard change had been and how little hope they had in the future. Most were waiting for the next reorg to be announced.

I didn't try to convince any of them to stay. That is not the role of a professional coach. What I did instead was help them move beyond their wounds by listening carefully to them. And then I guided each one to imagine a better future for themselves. I made it very clear that whatever future they envisioned didn't have to be at their current employer. (I'm not sure the Chief Marketing Officer would have been happy to hear I even mentioned the option of quitting, so I never told him.)

Over the course of a few months, the team began to heal. They brought up the past less frequently and began to focus on what was possible. Each person's vision was different; each possessed different values and strengths.

After six months, only one person resigned. The rest discovered they could still succeed despite it all.

In the final coaching sessions, I asked each person pointedly, "Do you choose to stay?" One or two said the "jury is still out," but the rest said yes.

Should You Resign?

Why am I sharing this story? It is to let you know that even if you think you've tried everything, you haven't. You only see the options you've always seen. That's what a coach is for. Through careful listening and insightful questions, we help you discover what you're missing. And often, those options are right in front of you. You may have other options to make things better at work—you just don't see them yet.

I'm also sharing this story to help you see that success that really matters is possible even in the most challenging of situations. John McCain survived every day of his captivity—his version of success. My first client group did more than survive; they found a way to win, each in their way. Getting clear on your vision, values, and strengths keeps you feeling accomplished every day.

Remember my client Eric? He was determined to get a seat on the leadership team. His vision was to contribute to company-wide decisions from his unique perspective as head of Quality and Regulatory. He did achieve his goal.

But he had to quit to get it.

Eric and I had discussed resignation as an option, but it was not something he was ready to do right away. Or at least that's what we both thought at the time.

Between our coaching sessions, Eric met with his immediate supervisor, who had advised him to abandon the idea of joining the leadership team. Eric's plan for this meeting was to review his assigned goals, update his boss as to his progress, and identify new quarterly objectives. Unfortunately, his boss appeared distracted, gave him the very same goals for next quarter, and cut the meeting short. Eric decided in that moment that he needed to act.

Eric went home, wrote a letter of resignation, and sent it to his boss and the CEO. The CEO was furious. "Get him back!"

Eric didn't take his resignation lightly. He had been interviewing with other organizations, and he had an offer on the table that he was barely considering. It wasn't ideal, but he would be allowed greater influence at the new company. With an open mind, Eric listened to his supervisor's offer, which included a seat on the leadership team—the first time a head of Quality had ever been included. He agreed to stay.

This was not the easiest route to achieving a hidden metric. Eric took a huge gamble, and it paid off for him. Note that he used quitting as a last resort. Before that, he put in the hard work of strengthening his authenticity, creating and repairing relationships, and investigating other companies. Eric also got clear on what he wanted to create for himself—his vision. His values also kept him on track. Ultimately, when he felt his values would be compromised by sticking around where he was not appreciated, he made the decision to leave.

Should you leave your company? Most career coaches—who specialize in career development, job searches, resume writing, interview preparation, and salary negotiation—would say that it's best practice to resign only when you find something else that is so exciting you are compelled to go for it. Sticking with a bad, though not abusive, situation can prepare you to deal with a similar scenario should it arise in another organization. Ask yourself, "Have I resolved all I can? Is there more to learn before I clean out my desk and return my laptop?"

In Eric's situation, he had decided enough was enough; he had learned all he could, and he sensed nothing would change—unless he changed it.

Should You Rework Your Hidden Metrics?

The likelihood of you having done something wrong in the hidden metrics process is low. You created these hidden metrics for a reason. Your intuition and ideal self set you on this path, not your ego.

That said, if now you suspect your vision came from your ego and not your intuition, then yes, rewrite your goals to something that is genuinely, deeply, and powerfully meaningful to you.

The Coach's Secret

Coaches know from experience, their own and that of their clients, that whenever we operate from our ideal self and listen to that optimistic, benevolent voice, we are doing what is right for us. We also know that when you do what is right for you, sometimes big change is needed.

No one can tell you what to do, least of all a coach. You are the only one who can decide what is best for you. Listen to your inner sage and the right answer will become clear.

12
YOU CAN DO THIS!

The essence of coaching is about helping clients achieve a future they can only partially see right now. My job is to reveal, through being fully present and posing intuitive questions, what may be holding you back as well as anything that will accelerate you forward. My focus is always on you, to help you see that what your heart is telling you is right.

But only you can tell me what that is.

In *Hidden Metrics*, I've provided you with some guidance on how to hear what your ideal self is telling you and how to take that message and manifest it into something that matters.

When we get clear on that message, we feel compelled to make it happen. It's a natural thing. Like falling in love. As Harry says in *When Harry Met Sally*, "When you realize you want to spend the rest of your life with somebody, you want the rest of your life to start as soon as possible." That same feeling surfaces when you are finally clear on what your vision is. You want it to begin right away.

Your values, those beliefs that guide your behavior, decisions, and actions, keep you on the path. Whenever you feel the temptation to give up, let go, or deviate from your values, you will feel an uncomfortable emotional pull that will draw you back to center.

Finally, your skills, talents, and strengths will organically keep you energized along the way. When you apply them, you'll be rewarded with a frisson of energy that keeps you vibrant and happy.

The Coach's Secret

Coaches know you can do this. I believe it because I've seen it happen for over thirty years of coaching leaders like yourself. Now is a perfect time, just after your recent promotion, to make it happen. Now is the time to become the leader you always knew you could be.

YOUR HIDDEN METRICS WORKBOOK

Use the following pages to craft your hidden metrics.

DATE: ____

MY CONTEXT

Jot down notes about what is happening at work and anything relevant you want to remember. Think about any pain points you may have experienced in the last three to six months and how they may have affected your ability or desire to do your job. Also, include any successes that brought you satisfaction or fulfillment. You'll want to create more of these high points going forward.

____

____

____

____

____

____

____

____

____

____

____

MY MOTIVE

Select which motive is the best reason for keeping your hidden metrics hidden and jot down why you're choosing to keep them hidden.

☐ **Inability to Ask for Help:** I am concerned about asking for help either because I may be seen as incompetent or others will hold it against me or I may lose control over what I want to achieve.

____

____

____

____

☐ **Obsolete Mindsets and Behaviors:** I am determined to change the old mindsets and habits that slow me down.

____

____

____

____

☐ **Long-Term Goals:** My business goals will take years to fulfill so I need to find ways to stay inspired.

____

____

____

____

☐ **Confidential Feelings:** I don't want to have others making judgments about me or my goal.

____

____

____

____

☐ **Audacious Goals:** My goal is so big, I don't want to share it until I'm ready.

____

____

____

____

☐ **Feedback Isn't Relevant or Accurate:** The feedback I've gotten doesn't apply so I'm going to work on something that has real meaning for me.

____

____

____

____

I WANT TO LET GO OF. . . AND EMBRACE. . .

Record notes about what you need and want to let go of. Note what you want to embrace.

Let go of: Your Old Vision of Yourself
Embrace: Yourself as Leader

____

____

____

____

Let go of: Being Friends with Your Squad
Embrace: Member of a New Team

____

____

____

____

Let go of: Work Means Being in Action
Embrace: Building Quality Relationships

____

____

____

____

Let go of: Focusing on Your Development
Embrace: Celebrating Others' Growth

____

____

____

____

Let go of: Telling People What to Do
Embrace: Inspiring Others

____

____

____

____

Let go of: Old Mindsets about Emotions
Embrace: The Power of Emotions

____

____

____

____

Let go of: Day-to-Day Tasks
Embrace: A Strategic Mindset

____

____

____

____

Let go of: Old Mindset re: Meetings
Embrace: Being a Full Participant in Meetings

Let go of: Doing the Work
Embrace: Your Own Experience and Knowledge

Let go of: Being the Hero
Embrace: Protecting Your Time

Let go of: Having All the Answers
Embrace: Enjoying the Mystery

Let go of: Making Decisions on Your Own
Embrace: Proactively Managing Risk

Let go of: Your Preferred Communication Style
Embrace: The Power of Language

Let go of: Leading Projects
Embrace: Leading People

Let go of: Pleasing Everyone
Embrace: Positive Results

WHERE ARE YOU IN YOUR TRANSITION?

Get a sense of where you are in the transition process.

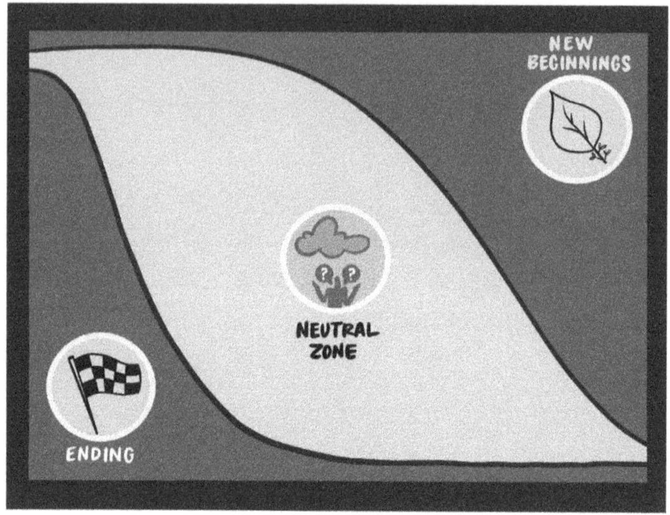

The Transition Model

Phase 1: Endings

Think about those things that you will no longer be responsible for.

1. What is ending for you?

____

____

____

____

2. What can you do to mark your Ending? What ritual or ceremony will help you move forward?

____

____

____

____

Phase 2: Neutral Zone

Track some of the questions that remain open for you as you move through the Neutral Zone. Note any progress you might have. Be sure to revisit this page as more questions surface and as you make progress.

✓ Unanswered Question

____

____

Notes on Progress or Resolution

____

____

____

____

____

✓ Unanswered Question

____

____

Notes on Progress or Resolution

____

____

____

____

____

✓ Unanswered Question

____

____

Notes on Progress or Resolution

____

____

____

____

____

____

✓ Unanswered Question

____

____

Notes on Progress or Resolution

____

____

____

____

____

____

✓ Unanswered Question

____

____

Notes on Progress or Resolution

____

____

____

____

____

____

Create a file or use additional sheets of paper should you have more unanswered questions.

Additional Neutral Zone Questions to Consider:

✓ What can you do to reassure yourself and others that you will find the answers you need?

____

____

____

____

____

____

✓ What can you do to celebrate the small wins during this ambiguous phase of transition?

____

____

____

____

Phase 3: New Beginnings

✓ What are some indicators that you are in the New Beginnings phase? What is working well right now?

____

____

____

____

✓ What accomplishments are you ready to celebrate?

____

____

____

____

✓ What can you do to mark this beginning? New swag? Lunch with the squad?

____

____

____

____

✓ What is still unanswered from the Neutral Zone?

____

____

____

____

✓ How will these items be resolved?

____

____

____

____

Relationship with Your Supervisor

✓ How would you describe your relationship with your supervisor?

____

____

____

____

✓ What works in your relationship with your supervisor?

____

____

____

____

____

✔ How could your relationship with your supervisor improve?

____

____

____

____

____

____

TRUST EQUATION

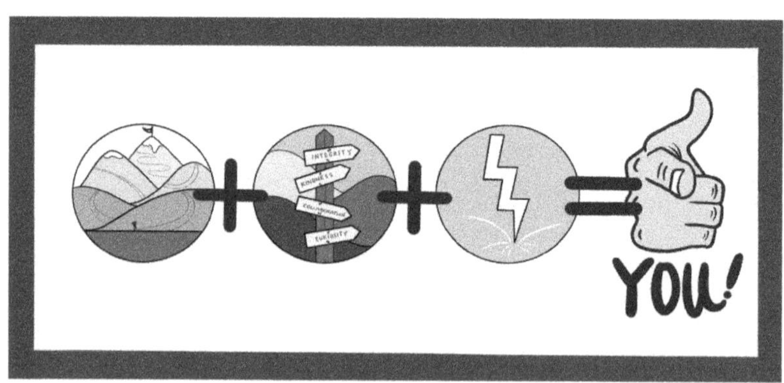

The Trust Equation

Using the Trust Equation, how trustworthy are you?

✔ Credibility =

✔ Reliability =

✔ Intimacy =

✔ Self-Orientation =

Calculate the Trust Quotient: _______________________________

✔ How can you improve your trustworthiness?

____

____

____

____

____

____

____

____

✔ How would you assess your supervisor's trustworthiness?

____

____

____

____

____

____

____

____

MY VISION STATEMENT

Write your vision statement here. Be sure to compose it in present tense, make it inspiring to you, and be as detailed as you can.

MY RALLYING CRY

Record the short version of your vision here. Make it easy to remember and inspiring.

HIDDEN METRICS VALUES:

DECISION-MAKING

Accountability | Competence | Confidence | Critical Thinking | Data Analysis | Decisive Action | Goal Setting | Initiative | Judgment | Problem Solving | Responsibility | Strategic Thinking | Wisdom

MENTOR/DEVELOP OTHERS

Accountability | Caring | Competence | Generosity | Growth | Learning | Patience | Service | Teaching | Wisdom

EMOTIONAL INTELLIGENCE

Compassion | Confidence | Emotional Regulation | Empathy | Grace | Humility | Patience | Present Focus | Respect | Self-Awareness | Self-Discipline | Self-Expression | Social Skills | Understanding | Vulnerability

INFLUENCE

Caring | Charisma | Clarity | Competence | Confidence | Critical Thinking | Humor | Inspiration | Persuasion | Presence | Recognition | Social Skills | Understanding | Vulnerability

RELATIONSHIPS

Belonging | Caring | Collaboration | Community | Compassion | Connection | Curiosity | Diversity | Empathy | Friendliness | Inclusion | Love | Loyalty | Respect

MEANING

Altruism | Ambition | Connection | Continuous Learning | Faith | Hope | Legacy | Loyalty | Love | Making a Difference | Purpose | Respect | Spirituality | Vision

ADAPTABILITY

Agility | Continuous Learning | Creativity | Curiosity | Flexibility | Growth Mindset | Innovation | Resilience

ETHICS

Corporate Responsibility | Dignity | Ethics | Fairness | Honest | Integrity | Justice | Respect | Responsibility | Social Responsibility | Stewardship | Transparency | Trustworthiness

FEEDBACK

Active Listening | Ambition | Caring | Continuous Learning | Curiosity | Factualness | Growth Mindset | Honesty | Receptiveness

DELEGATION

Accountability | Communication | Confidence | Empowerment | Growth Mindset | Responsibility | Trustworthiness

COMMUNICATION

Active Listening | Assertiveness | Authenticity | Clarity | Compassion | Conciseness | Honesty | Truth | Understanding

BUSINESS ACUMEN

Achievement | Competence | Competition | Customer Focus | Efficiency | Excellence | Financial Security | Innovation | Resourcefulness | Strategic Thinking | Success | Wealth

SOCIAL RESPONSIBILITY

Citizenship | Community Service | Environment | Generosity

SECURITY

Consistency | Protection | Reliability | Risk | Safety | Security | Stability

PERSONAL EXCELLENCE

Ambition | Commitment | Determination | Discipline | Perseverance | Work-Life Balance

EXECUTIVE PRESENCE

Accountability | Charisma | Confidence | Excellence | Honesty | Respect | Trustworthiness

STRATEGIC CAPABILITIES

Ambition | Big Picture Focus | Collaboration | Continuous | Learning | Critical Thinking | Data Analysis | Future Orientation | Growth Mindset | Innovation | Long-Term Vision Risk

MY VALUES

Write down the values you will use to keep you on your path to Vision. Select ten, then narrow your list to five. Add notes describing what the value means to you.

1. ____

____

2. ____

____

3. ____

____

4. ____

____

5. ____

____

6. ____

____

7. ____

____

8. ____

____

9. ____

____

10. ____

____

MY STRENGTHS

Jot down those strengths that you perform well and energize you and will help you achieve your vision.

1. ____

____

2. ____

____

3. ____

____

4. ____

____

5. ____

____

6. ____

____

7. ____

____

8. ____

____

9. ____

____

10. ____

____

CAPPFINITY SKILLS

✓ **Being:** Our way of being in the world

Authenticity – You are always true to yourself, even in the face of pressure.

Centered – You have an inner composure and self-assurance, whatever the situation.

Courage – You overcome your fears and do what you want to do in spite of them.

Credibility – You gain the confidence and trust of others with your professionalism.

Curiosity – You are interested in everything, always seeking out new information.

Gratitude – You are constantly thankful for the positive things in your life.

Humility – You stay in the background, giving others credit for your contributions.

Legacy – You love to create things that will outlast you and are sustainable.

Mission – You pursue things which give you a sense of meaning and purpose.

Moral Compass – You strive to act in accordance with what you believe is right.

Personal Responsibility – You take ownership of your decisions and are always accountable.

Pride – You strive to produce work that is of the highest standard and quality.

Service – You are constantly looking for ways to serve and help others.

Self-Awareness – You know yourself well, understanding your own emotions and behavior.

Unconditionality – You accept people for who they are, without ever needing to judge them.

✔ **Communicating**: How we give and receive information

Counterpoint – You always bring a different viewpoint to others, whatever the context.

Customer Champion – You love to represent customers' and stakeholders' interests.

Explainer – You easily simplify things so that others can understand.

Feedback – You provide fair and accurate feedback so others can develop.

Humor – You see the funny side of almost everything—and make a joke of it.

Listener – You love to focus on and listen intently to what people say.

Narrator – You love to tell stories and see the power of them to convey insights.

Social Adaptability – You naturally adapt your behavior to different social situations.

Spotlight – You love to be the focus of everyone's attention by speaking up.

Writer – You love to write, conveying thoughts and ideas in the written word.

✔ **Motivating**: Our drive towards action

Action – You feel compelled to act immediately and decisively.

Adventure – You love to take risks and stretch yourself outside your comfort zone.

Bounceback – You use setbacks as springboards to go on and achieve even more.

Catalyst – You love to motivate and inspire others to make things happen.

Change Agent – You are always involved with change by advocating and making it happen.

Collaboration – You enjoy achieving results by working as part of a team.

Commercial Insight – You are focused on bottom-line impact and commercial success.

Competitive – You are always competing to win, wanting to perform better than others.

Drive – You are very self-motivated and push yourself hard.

Growth – You always look for ways to grow and develop, whatever you are doing.

Implementer – You love to turn ideas and plans into practical solutions.

Improver – You constantly look for better ways of doing things.

Initiative – You take the initiative and make decisions, to get things started.

Learning Agility – You learn things quickly, applying your learning in new situations.

Opportunity Spotter – You consistently find and grasp new opportunities as they arise.

Persistence – You achieve success by keeping going, even when things are difficult.

Pace – You love to work at pace, getting things done quickly.

Performance Focus – You enjoy ensuring people deliver performance.

Resilience – You take hardships in your stride, recovering quickly and moving on.

Self-Belief – You are confident in your abilities, knowing you can achieve your goals.

Work Ethic – You are very hard working, putting a lot of effort into everything.

✔ **Thinking:** Our approach to situations

Adaptable – You love to meet changing demands and find the best fit.

Adherence – You love to follow processes, operating firmly within rules.

Analysis – You love to analyse things, working out what is happening and why.

Business Thinker – You have a keen interest in business, understanding how it operates.

Creativity – You strive to produce original work by combining things imaginatively.

Detail – You naturally focus on the small things that others easily miss.

Diligence – You stay focused on repetitive tasks, double-checking things.

Incisive – You instinctively see through complexity to identify the key issues.

Incubator – You love to think deeply about things to arrive at the best conclusion.

Innovation – You approach things in ingenious and new ways.

Optimism – You always maintain a positive attitude and outlook on life.

Orchestrator – You like to co-ordinate people and resources to get things done.

Organizer – You are exceptionally well-organized in everything you do.

Planner – You make plans for everything you do, covering all eventualities.

Prevention – You think ahead, to anticipate and prevent problems before they happen.

Resolver – You love to solve problems, the more difficult the better.

Strategic Awareness – You pay attention to the wider factors and bigger picture.

Technology Focus – You focus on technology, keeping up-to-date with new developments.

Time Optimizer – You maximize your time, to get the most out of the time you have available.

Judgment – You enjoy making decisions and can make the right decision quickly.

✓ **Relating:** How we relate to others

Approachable – You are open and accessible, readily approachable to others.

Compassion – You really care about others, doing all you can to help and sympathize.

Connector – You spot connections between people, making links and introductions.

Emotional Awareness – You are acutely aware of the emotions and feelings of others.

Empathic – You feel connected to others by understanding what they are feeling.

Enabler – You create the conditions for people to grow and develop for themselves.

Esteem Builder – You love to help others to believe in themselves.

Equality – You ensure that everyone is treated equally and pay attention to fairness.

Inclusion – You ensure people are included and feel part of the group or team.

Persuasion – You enjoy bringing others round to your way of thinking.

Personalization – You recognize everyone as unique, noticing their subtle differences.

Rapport Builder – You establish rapport and relationships with others quickly and easily.

Relationship Deepener – You have a natural ability to form deep, long lasting relationships.

Relationship Manager – You build and maintain relationships with people to achieve objectives.

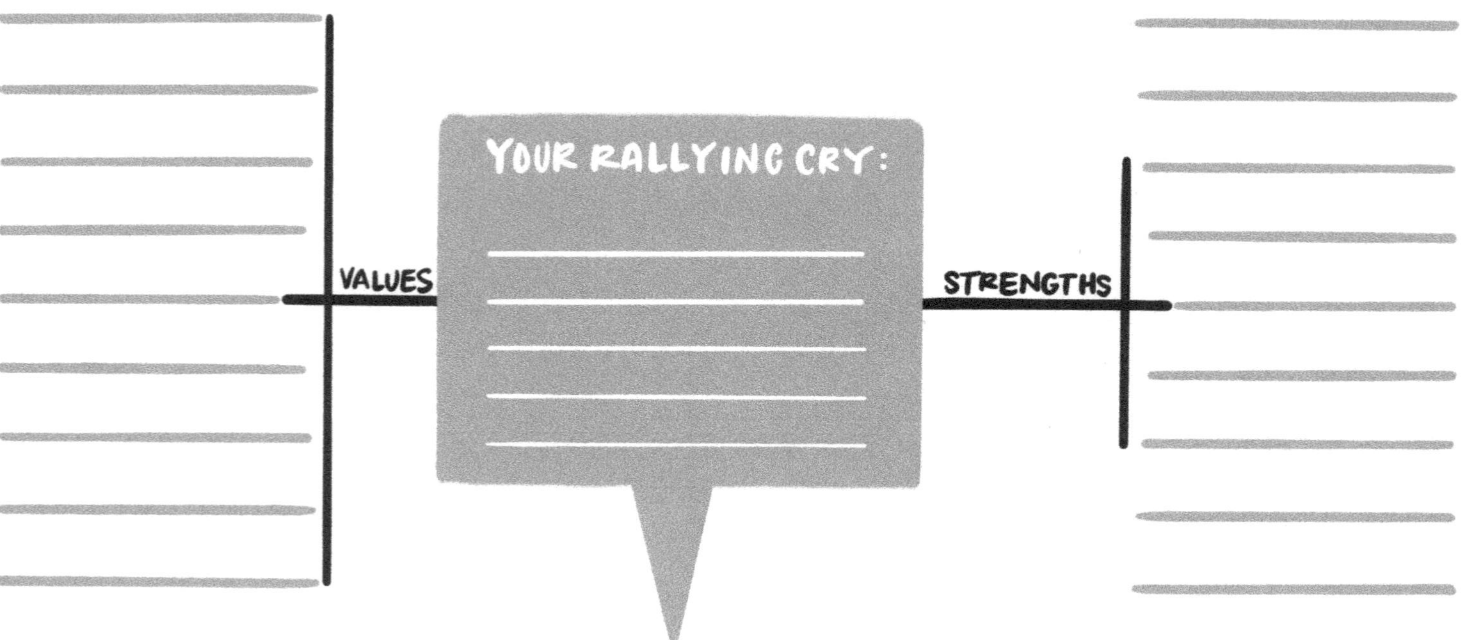

YOUR RALLYING CRY:
VALUES
STRENGTHS

MY HIDDEN METRICS

Record your metrics here to track your progress. Be sure to revisit this page as you progress on your goals.

✓ Key Actions to Take:

____

____

____

____

Relevant Values and Strengths:

____

____

____

Deadline:

____

✓ Key Actions to Take:

____

____

____

____

Relevant Values and Strengths:

____

____

____

Deadline:

____

✓ Key Actions to Take:

____

____

____

Relevant Values and Strengths:

____

____

____

Deadline:

____

✓ Key Actions to Take:

____

____

____

Relevant Values and Strengths:

____

____

____

Deadline:

____

✓ Key Actions to Take:

____

____

____

____

Relevant Values and Strengths:

____

____

____

Deadline:

____

✓ Key Actions to Take:

____

____

____

____

Relevant Values and Strengths:

____

____

____

____

Deadline:

____

MY RESULTS

Document and celebrate your results.

____

____

____

____

____

____

____

____

____

____

____

____

____

____

____

**CONGRATULATIONS! WAY TO GO! YAHOO!
NOW, GO OUT AND MAKE IT HAPPEN!**

BIBLIOGRAPHY

A Meaning of Life.org. "The 4 Cornerstones of Meaning." Randall Grayson, PhD, https://ameaningoflife.org/cornerstones-of-meaning/. Accessed June 20, 2025.

Body, Emotion, Language Model. *Coaching for Personal and Professional Mastery*, 1999. The Newfield Network Training Materials.

Boyatzis, Richard, PhD. *The Science of Change: Discovering Sustained, Desired Change from Individuals to Organizations and Communities.* Oxford University Press, 2024.

Bridges, William. *Managing Transitions, Making the Most of Change.* Da Cape Lifelong Books, 25tth Anniversary Edition, 2017.

Brown, Brené. *Dare to Lead: Brave Work, Tough Conversations, Whole Hearts.* Random House Publishing, 2018.

Cohen, Allan R., and David L. Bradford. *Influence without Authority.* 3rd ed., Wiley, 2017.

BIBLIOGRAPHY

Chartered Management Institute. *Taking Responsibility—Why UK PLC Needs Better Managers.* https://www.managers.org.uk/wp-content/uploads/2023/10/CMI_BMB_GoodManagment_Report.pdf. 2023.

Edelman. *2024 Edelman Trust Barometer,* https://www.edelman.com/trust/2024/trust-barometer/special-report-trust-at-work. 2024.

Emerald, David. *The Power of TED** (The Empowerment Dynamic). Center for the Empowerment Dynamic, 2016.

Feltman, Charles. *The Thin Book of Trust: An Essential Primer for Building Trust at Work.* Thin Book Publishing, 2009.

Gallup Business Journal. Beck, Randall and Harter, Jim. *Managers Account for 70% of Variance in Employee Engagement.* April 21, 2015.

Goldsmith, Marshall. *What Got You Here Won't Get You There: How Successful People Become Even More Successful.* New York: Hyperion, 2007.

Gallup.com/Cliftonstrengths. *StrengthsFinder.* https://www.gallup.com/cliftonstrengths/en/252137/home.aspx. Accessed June 22, 2025.

Karpman, Stephen B. MD. (2014). *A Game Free Life: The New Transactional Analysis of Intimacy, Openness, and Happiness.* San Francisco: Drama Triangle Publications.

Klaver [Bouchard], M. Nora. *Mayday! Asking for Help in Times of Need.* San Francisco: Berrett-Koehler Publishers, 2007.

Linley, Alex, and Bateman, Janet. Strengths *Profile Book: Finding What You Can Do and Love to Do and Why It Matters.* Capp Press, 2018.

Maister, David H., Green, Charles H., and Galford, Robert M., *The Trusted Advisor.* The Free Press, 2001 and 2021.

Muller, Jerry Z. *The Tyranny of Metrics.* Princeton: Princeton University Press, 2018.

Newby, Dan, and Watkins, Curtis. *The Field Guide to Emotions: A Practical Orientation to 150 Essential Emotions.* Daniel Newby, 2019.

VIAcharacter.org. *VIA Inventory of Strengths.* https://www.viacharacter.org/. Accessed June 22, 2025. VIA Inventory of Strengths (VIA-IS-P) McGrath, R. E. (2019). Technical report: The VIA Assessment Suite for Adults: Development and initial evaluation (rev. ed.). VIA Institute on Character, www.viacharacter.org

IN GRATITUDE

I am indebted to so many people who helped me write and produce *Hidden Metrics*. I am continually amazed at how, when my vision for this book became clear to me, all of the talented people I needed to help me edit, review, style, illustrate, and market the book showed up out of nowhere. I am deeply grateful to them all.

Let me begin by thanking all my clients, those who showed up in the pages of this book and those who did not. Your willingness to play, stretch, and challenge yourselves inspires me every day. Thank you for trusting me with your visions and secrets. Special notice goes to Erin Spaulding, who inspired me to write this book. As we worked together to manifest her vision, the process flowed and the work I've been doing for years became clearer. The hidden metrics approach became crystal clear.

Next, appreciation goes to my coaching sisters: Susan Spritz-Myers, Molly Sullivan, Orla Castanien, Colleen Boselli, and Rosemarie Perla. Powerful coaches and brilliant women in your own right, each of you has contributed to the success of this book. Susan, you spur me on, encouraging me and challenging me in equal amounts. Orla, thank you for being my coach and introducing me to the Realise2! Colleen, your ability to manifest blows me away. You are a role-model in making things happen. Rosemarie, I so appreciate your soft yet direct approach to providing ideas and feedback. It's helped make my writing so much better. Every author needs someone who has her back—that's you, Molly! Thank you for being there for me!

Next, my friend and colleague, Sunshine Ben BelKacem, a brilliant artist and graphic facilitator. Your intuition flows through your pen, making everything easier to understand. The icon and illustrations bring *Hidden Metrics* alive! Thank you!

To my team of editors: Taylor Maccoux, for being a perfect client and resource. I'm grateful you introduced me to Erin McClary, editor extraordinaire. Your work is "superb"! I'm so glad you understand my audience as well as I do. I'm grateful to Laura Matthews, of thinkStory.biz who made sure each sentence made sense and forced me to curtail my use of exclamation marks!!! Also, thank you to Elsa Safir for your artistry in making this book beautiful, accessible, and easy to read.

Elissa Blankenship, my brilliant and intuitive friend, I owe you a debt for helping me get the word out about *Hidden Metrics*. I love how we've connected. Makes me wonder from which past life we knew each other. Thank you.

I can't forget Don Grady. I have no doubt your spirit has been hanging around and encouraging me while I wrote this book. Thank you for the laughter, lessons, and wisdom.

I also owe my husband, Peter, a debt of gratitude that is forever. Your support during long days of writing, alone in my office without an extra chair. Thank you for your support during long days of writing, alone in my office without an extra chair, for manning up, loving me, and being by my side through it all.

ABOUT THE AUTHOR

M. Nora Bouchard, MA, PCC, brings three decades of expertise to executive and leadership coaching, helping leaders at every level—from emerging talent to C-suite executives—develop the skills and presence needed to lead with impact and authenticity.

As a certified coach through both the Newfield Network and the International Coach Federation, Nora combines rigorous training with deep practical experience. Her approach focuses on designing sustainable leadership practices that create lasting organizational change. She is an active member of the Institute of Coaching and AMeaningOfLife.org, staying connected to the latest developments in leadership psychology and human potential.

Nora is the author of *Mayday! Asking for Help in Times of Need*, published by Berrett-Koehler Publishing, where she explores the courage and wisdom required to seek support during challenging times—a skill essential for effective leadership. Nora's guided meditations can also be found on AuraHealth.io.

When she's not coaching leaders or speaking to organizations, Nora enjoys life in Oak Park, Illinois, with her husband Peter and their beloved pooch Cole.

To learn more about working with Nora or having her speak to your organization, visit https://www.mnorabouchard.com.